MW01103318

AutoCAD R13 Essentials

Melton M. Miller
Department of Civil Engineering
University of Massachusetts at Amherst

Addison-Wesley Publishing Company, Inc.
Menlo Park, California · Reading, Massachusetts
New York · Don Mills, Ontario · Harlow, U.K. · Amsterdam
Bonn · Paris · Milan · Madrid · Sydney · Singapore · Tokyo
Seoul · Taipei · Mexico City · San Juan, Puerto Rico

Copyright © 1997 by Addison-Wesley Publishing
Company, Inc.

All rights reserved. No part of this publication
may be reproduced, stored in a retrieval system, or
transmitted, in any form or by any means, electronic,
mechanical, photocopying, recording, or any other
media or embodiments now known or hereafter to
become known, without the prior written permission
of the publisher. Printed in the United States of
America. Published simultaneously in Canada.

The applications and examples presented in this
book have been included for their instructional
value. They have been tested with care but are not
guaranteed for any particular purpose. The publisher
does not offer any warranties or representations,
nor does it accept any liabilities with respect to the
applications and examples.

AutoCAD, AutoSketch and Autodesk are registered
trademarks of Autodesk, Inc. Some of the product
names used herein have been used for identification
purposes only and may be trademarks of their
respective companies.

This is a module in the *Engineer's Toolkit*, an
Addison-Wesley SELECT edition. Contact your sales
representative for more information.

The Engineer's Toolkit and SELECT are trademarks
of Addison-Wesley Publishing Company, Inc.

Photo Credits:
Chapter 1: Courtesy of Autodesk, Inc.
Chapter 2: ©Peter Menzel
Chapter 3: Courtesy of 3M
Chapter 4: ©Walter Urie/Westlight
Chapter 5: ©Jeff Greenberg/Photo Researchers, Inc.
Chapter 6: ©Tim Davis/Photo Researchers, Inc.

ISBN: 0-8053-6422-6

Addison-Wesley Publishing Company, Inc.
2725 Sand Hill Road
Menlo Park, CA 94025
http://www.aw.com/cseng/toolkit/

Contents

1 Tackling Design Problems with AutoCAD

Computer-aided Design Drawings are a critical medium of communication for professionals in fields as diverse as engineering, landscape architecture, and the theater. Engineers, landscape architects, and theatrical set designers all rely on graphic presentations to communicate their designs to those who bring the designs to life. As relatively new arrivals in the field of engineering, computer-aided design (CAD) programs aid immeasurably in the design process. Using CAD programs, you can design and view your models on the screen, easily making modifications and then printing or plotting your design only when it is just right. CAD programs simplify the design of projects as straightforward as a bird house and as complex as a space shuttle. Even a sophisti-

cated CAD program can't do all your work for you, however. You still need to plan ahead and hone your problem-solving skills. This chapter introduces you to a five-step problem-solving strategy to help you do just that.

INTRODUCTION

This chapter introduces the AutoCAD program, explains the types of design problems it is equipped to solve, and lays out a five-step approach for solving a wide range of design problems. It also illustrates this five-step process by describing how to draw a bolt-and-nut assembly.

1-1 CAD SYSTEMS AND AUTOCAD

Simply put, computer-aided design (CAD) programs enable you to draw objects using your computer and view them on the screen. Before the advent of computers and CAD programs, design calculations were done with what now seem to be very primitive tools, including slide rules, triangles, T-squares, erasers, and pencils. Creating drawings was a labor-intensive process, and making modifications was time-consuming. Fortunately, these old tools have been replaced with hand-held calculators and personal computers (PCs). Now that PCs are relatively inexpensive, you can generate your drawings with an easy-to-use program. CAD programs enable you to draw with extreme accuracy, save your drawings in files, and later retrieve and modify them as needed. You no longer need an eraser. The process of making changes to a drawing has become as straightforward as the drawing process itself. You are also able to organize your drawing files into directories or jobs for management of large projects. This feature is especially helpful when you are working with multiple assemblies and with other design team members. When you have finalized the design and completed the drawings, you can then plot or print the finished drawings.

AutoCAD is one of the most widely used CAD software packages. It provides you with commands in a menu format and supplies prompts to guide you through the drawing process. The prompts will ask you for the specific information needed to execute the command you have chosen. AutoCAD doesn't do your thinking for you, however. Regardless of how easy and powerful the program may be, you still must have a plan of action before launching into a drawing. As mentioned, this chapter introduces a five-step process that will help you plan your drawings. An intelligent programmer does not begin writing code for a program in FORTRAN or Pascal without first developing an algorithm. Neither should an AutoCAD user begin a drawing without a plan.

You may have heard about the AutoSketch program, and you might be curious about how it differs from AutoCAD. Although AutoCAD and AutoSketch have many common features, AutoSketch is limited to two-dimensional views. In contrast, with AutoCAD you can draw objects in three dimensions and view those objects from any angle.

Most schools or colleges have set up local area networks (LANs) that support a number of PCs. Chances are that you will be using AutoCAD within such an environment. These personal computers are actually workstations connected to a fileserver, which functions as one large hard drive for all the workstations. When you turn on the PC and connect to the fileserver through a login process, you have gained access to the software on the fileserver. (Depending on your privileges as a network user, you may not have access to everything on the fileserver.) The PCs are "intelli-

2 Getting Started with AutoCAD

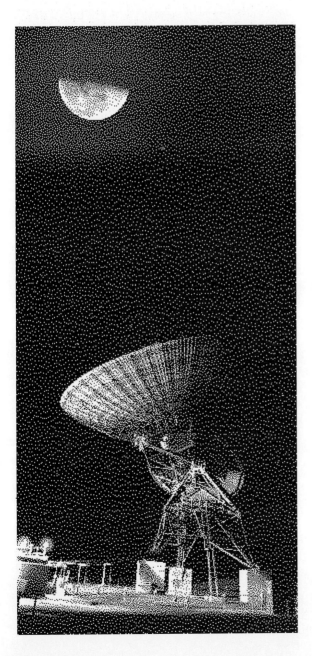

Application Satellites

Application satellites relay information ranging from communication signals to weather information.

The data collected by application satellites is relayed to the earth and collected by satellite dishes. These dishes, in turn, transmit the data to a network of other receivers. The common satellite dish is constructed as a network of structural ribs connected by plates. The geometry of the dish—the number of ribs and the angle between them—is used to design the connecting plate.

Buckminster Fuller's geodesic dome is another three-dimensional structure made up of ribs connected by plates. A geodesic dome is spherical in shape, but the surface is actually made up of a series of interconnected polygons rather than one sphere. Geodesic domes are used to protect satellite radio telescopes, satellite dishes, and other sensitive equipment. At the end of this chapter, you will draw a connecting plate for a geodesic dome.

INTRODUCTION

This chapter introduces some basic features of the AutoCAD program. You will learn how to start the program and how to identify and use the various elements of the screen. You will also learn some simple drawing techniques and use a few easy editing tools. Throughout the text you can test your understanding of what you have learned by doing the Try It! exercises. You should read this module while you are sitting at a computer and trying these exercises. The more you experiment, the more quickly you will learn AutoCAD. It is assumed that you have no previous experience with AutoCAD but some experience with PCs.

2-1 STARTING AUTOCAD

To start AutoCAD, you simply double-click the AutoCAD icon shown in Figure 2-1. If the AutoCAD icon does not appear on your system, check with your system administrator or your instructor about how to start the software on your system. As it starts, AutoCAD displays some information, and then the drawing area appears.

Figure 2-1
AutoCAD Icon

Try It

Turn on the computer and start AutoCAD so you can follow along as you read this chapter.

2-2 EXPLORING THE AUTOCAD INTERFACE

This section explores various aspects of the AutoCAD interface. First you will learn a bit about the input devices you will use to communicate with AutoCAD. Next you will be introduced to the various components of the drawing screen. You will also learn how to use the various types of AutoCAD menus.

Using Input Devices

Communication with any applications package requires the use of input devices. The most common input device is the keyboard. In some situations when using AutoCAD, you must use the keyboard as the input device. For example, you may be required to supply the coordinates of a point in response to a command prompt. Remember that the computer cannot register the information until you press (ENTER). You can also use special *function keys*—including (F1), (F6), (F7), (F8), and (F9)—to implement AutoCAD features. Function keys will be discussed as needed throughout this module.

The other common input device is the *mouse.* You use the mouse to choose items from menus and to select or pick specific points or objects on the screen. Moving the mouse on the pad changes the screen position of the pointer. When the pointer is in the correct location, you quickly press the left button on the mouse to choose a menu option or select an object or point on the screen. Pressing the left mouse button to select objects on a drawing or items on a menu or dialog box is often called clicking. The right mouse button (on a three-button mouse) functions in the same way as the (ENTER) key. That is, if you press the right mouse button, AutoCAD responds as if you had pressed the (ENTER) key.

Although some AutoCAD installations require another type of input device called a digitizing tablet, in this text you will use only a mouse and keyboard.

Exploring the Drawing Screen

When you start AutoCAD you see a drawing screen like the one in Figure 2-2. The various parts of the screen are labeled in Figure 2-2 and are described below. Note that your default screen appearance may vary somewhat from that shown in the figure.

Figure 2-2
Drawing Screen

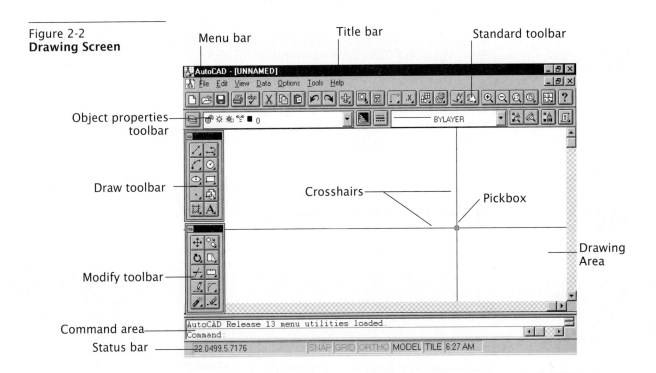

Drawing Area   The *drawing area* is the blank area that occupies most of the screen. It is in this region that you will be making your actual drawings. The lower-left corner of the drawing area is the origin (0,0) of the coordinate axes, although the origin is not shown on the screen.

Crosshairs and Pickbox   The *crosshairs* are the vertical and horizontal lines that extend across the entire drawing area. As you move the mouse, the cross-hairs move with it. You use the crosshairs to help you line things up properly on your drawing. At their intersection is a small rectangle called the *pickbox*, which you can use to select objects on the screen. The pickbox may not be shown in your default AutoCAD display. When executing some editing commands the pickbox will change appearance and will then be known as the aperture. You control the position of the crosshairs and pickbox by moving the mouse.

Title Bar   The *title bar* across the top of the screen displays the name of the drawing you are currently working on. Until you save your work and give it a descriptive name, the title bar displays a title of Unnamed, as seen in Figure 2-2. The title bar also indicates the number of currently open AutoCAD drawings.

Command Area   Directly below the drawing area is the *command area*, which consists of two lines of text. The lower line of the two is the *command line*. When the word "Command" appears on the second line in this area, AutoCAD is ready to receive a command. You can enter a command from the keyboard or select a command from a menu. The upper line of the command line displays the most recently executed command. Any prompts requesting data are displayed on the command line.

Menu Bar   Most of the menu options you will need to create and edit your AutoCAD drawing will be found in the options listed on the *menu bar*. To access one of the options from these menus, you merely point to the correct menu item and click the mouse button.

Status Bar   The *status bar* across the bottom of the screen displays useful information such as the X,Y location of the pickbox (22.0499,5.7176 in Figure 2-2) as well as the current time. Other information regarding your current drawing mode is also displayed on the status bar. The status bar also acts as a menu for options such as Snap, Grid and Ortho. You will learn about some of these options later in this module.

Toolbars   Four *toolbars* are displayed on the screen by default. Each toolbar contains buttons that, when selected, initiate commands. Displayed horizontally below the menu bar are the Standard toolbar and the Object Properties toolbar. The Standard toolbar contains buttons for saving a drawing, printing, cutting, pasting, copying, and so on. You use the Object Properties toolbar to obtain information regarding the drawing layer and its attributes. The Draw and Modify toolbars are displayed vertically along the left side of the drawing screen. They contain the buttons you need to draw and edit on the screen. If you point to one of the buttons on the toolbars, the function of that button will be displayed for you. Using toolbars to execute commands is described in the next section.

Try It
- Move the crosshairs around the drawing area. Notice how the coordinate display changes as you move the crosshairs.
- Move the crosshairs into the menu bar and click any item.
- Point to one of the buttons on the Modify toolbar and wait for the button function to be displayed.

Initiating Commands

AutoCAD provides three means of initiating commands: menus, toolbars, and the command line. Some commands can only be initiated from either a menu or a toolbar and some are available on both, but you can initiate any command from the command line.

Using Menus   When you choose an item from the menu bar, a pull-down menu appears, displaying a series of options. You select an item from the pull-down menu by moving the mouse up or down to highlight your choice and then clicking. When you select a pull-down menu option marked with a solid triangle (▶), another submenu appears, offering more options. Figure 2-3 shows the Tools pull-down menu with the Toolbars submenu displayed. Selecting a pull-down menu item marked with an ellipsis (...) opens a *dialog box.* You complete the execution of the command by entering values and/or choosing options in the dialog box. You will use many dialog boxes throughout this text .

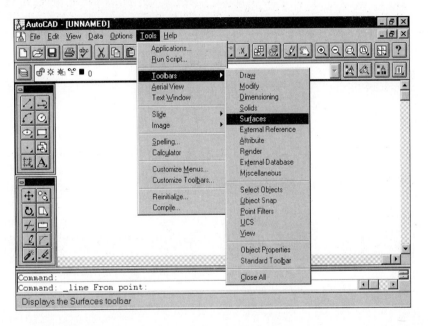

Figure 2-3
**A Typical Pull-down Menu
and Associated Submenu**

Using Toolbars   You select a toobar button by pointing to it and clicking. A button with a solid triangle in the lower-right corner provides access to more buttons displayed on a graphical pop-up menu. To access a graphical pop-up menu, point to the toolbar button and hold down the left mouse button. When the pop-up menu appears, you can select one of its options by highlighting it and releasing the mouse button. Figure 2-4 shows the graphical pop-up menu that appears when you point to Line on the Draw toolbar.

Figure 2-4
**A Typical Graphical
Pop-up Menu and
Associated Submenu**

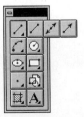

Try It

♦ Select View from the menu bar, and then select the Zoom option.
♦ Point to one of the buttons on the Draw toolbar and hold down to observe the graphical pop-up menu which appears.

Command Line   You can type in commands at the command line to initiate commands. Typically, this option will be utilized by more advanced users of AutoCAD. The first line of the command area displays the most recently selected command. To see previous commands which you issued, you will need to view the text screen. You press (F2) to switch between the drawing area and the text screen. As you enter commands and responses into the command area, the lines of text scroll upward. Only one line of text from the text screen is visible at any time directly above the Command line. The names of the commands that you choose are recorded in the text screen. You can click the up or down arrows at the end of the single line of the text screen to scroll through previous commands which you executed. To display the entire text screen and view the remainder of the text, press (F2). (Press (F2) again to toggle back to the drawing screen). This screen is useful if you want to review a sequence of the most recently executed commands and responses.

2-3   USING ON-LINE HELP

You can get information about AutoCAD commands by choosing **Help** from the menu bar. The pull-down menu shown in Figure 2-5 appears. To obtain information about a particular command, you select **Search for Help on** from this menu and type the name of the command in the dialog box that appears. There is also a list to scroll through that contains all of the available help topics. When you find the desired command, select it with the mouse and choose Display. The first page of help information

Figure 2-5
Help Pull-down menu

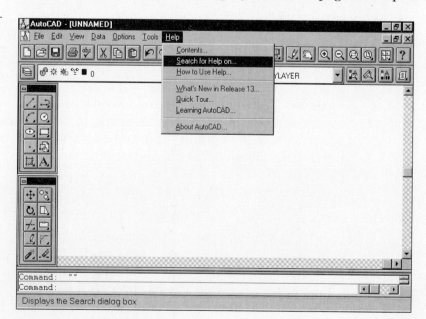

about that command appears. Use the Next and Previous arrows to move forward and backward through the pages of information. Finally, exit the Help command by selecting **Exit** from the **File** pull-down menu within the Help window (not the main AutoCAD window).

Try It

◆ Open the Help dialog box and get help on the Line command.
◆ Explore the contents of the Line Help window to see the large number of items you can get help with.

2-4 SETTING UP YOUR AUTOCAD DRAWING

Before you begin to draw, you must take two preparatory steps: select units and set the drawing limits. You also need to understand the AutoCAD coordinate system before you enter data for your drawing.

Selecting Units of Measurement

The type of units you choose depends on the kind of drawing you want to create. If you are drawing a machine part, you may need to use decimal units. If you are drawing a house, you should use architectural units. In other words, you should select units that are appropriate to the type of drawing you will create. Examples of the units of measurement used by AutoCAD are shown in Table 2-1. The examples illustrate the precision of the unit as well as the appearance of the text that will eventually appear in the drawing dimensions. Adding dimensions to drawings will be discussed in Chapter 5.

Table 2-1 AutoCAD Units of Measurement

Units	Example
Scientific	1.55E+01
Decimal	15.50
Engineering	1' – 3.50"
Architectural	1' – 3 1/2"
Fractional	15 1/2"

You can also control the direction of positive angles when setting the units. Positive angles are measured counterclockwise from the three o'clock position.

To select the units for your drawing, choose **Units** from the **Data** pull-down menu. The Units Control dialog box appears as shown in Figure 2-6. The choices for units and angles consist of columns of buttons. You click the button associated with the desired units to select them. The center of the button becomes filled in to indicate that it is selected. To select the number of decimal places, click the down arrow under Precision and pick the desired precision. You select the angular measure and precision in the same way. When you are satisfied with your selections, click OK. The dialog box disappears, and the crosshairs return. If you decide to cancel the command, click Cancel. If you want to set the direction of the angles, click Direction.

Figure 2-6
**Units Control
Dialog Box**

Try It

♦ Set the drawing units to Architectural.
♦ Move the crosshairs around the drawing area and notice how the coordinates are listed in the status bar.
♦ Restore the units to Decimal, and change the number of decimal places to 4.

Setting Drawing Limits

Before you begin a new drawing you should also set the limits of the screen. The limits are determined by the coordinates at both the lower-left corner and the upper-right corner of the screen. The default settings are 0,0 for the lower-left corner and 12,9 for the upper-right corner. The effect of the limits is easy to understand if you imagine drawing a simple rectangle using different limits. A rectangle that is 6 units wide and 4.5

Figure 2-7
**Rectangle (6 x 4.5 units)
with Default Limits 12,9**

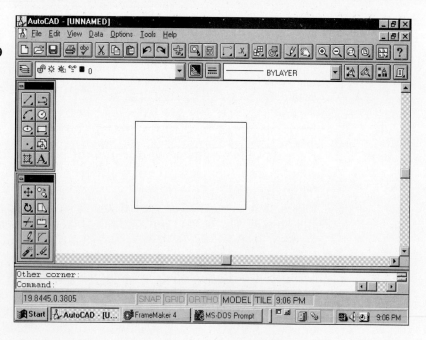

units high occupies one quarter of the screen area if the units are set to Decimal. In other words, the screen represents an approximate 12-by-9 decimal-unit rectangle. Figure 2-7 shows the rectangle drawn with the default limits. If you change the drawing limits—for example, change the upper limit to 24,18—without redrawing the rectangle and then view the entire drawing, it appears to be much smaller on the screen because it is a much smaller percentage of the entire drawing. Figure 2-8 shows the same rectangle using the new limits.

Figure 2-8
**Rectangle (6×4.5 units)
with Limits 24,18**

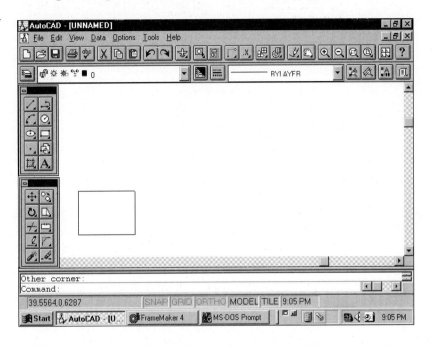

The drawing screen represents the space that you have available for your drawing. It is referred to as the model space, as opposed to the paper space on which the drawing will eventually be plotted. Objects drawn in the model space are always drawn full scale using the units selected for the drawing. When the drawings are plotted, the scale of the plot is adjusted so the drawing will fit on the paper. It is important that you scale the model space (that is, the drawing area) to fit the size of your drawing. For example, if the rectangle you are drawing represents a picture frame, you can use the default settings for the limits, and the image will fit on the screen easily. If, however, the rectangle is a drawing of the outline of a football stadium, you will need more model space to show the entire drawing on the screen. You will very likely change the drawing units to Engineering or Architectural and change the upper limit to 240,90 feet.

You change the limits of your drawing by choosing **Drawing Limits** from the **Data** pull-down menu. In the command area, the first prompt appears:

```
Reset Model space limits
ON/OFF/<Lower left corner> <0.0000,0.0000>:
```

You can accept the default coordinates by pressing (ENTER), or you can enter new values. (If you're using Engineering, Architectural, or Fractional units, AutoCAD assumes that the numbers you're entering represent inches. You can specify feet by entering the foot symbol, the apostrophe, after each coordinate.) The next prompt is

```
Upper right corner <12.0000,9.0000>:
```

Again, you can accept the default values or enter new values. If you expand the upper limits, the effect is not apparent until you extend your view to the new limits using the Zoom command. If you move the crosshairs to the upper-right corner of the screen, the coordinates of this point are the original upper limits. To fit the model space to the screen, choose **Zoom** from the **View** pull-down menu and then select **Limits**. Now the coordinate display shows the upper limits correctly. The Zoom command is discussed in more detail in Chapter 3.

You can set the Limits command on or off by choosing **Drawing Limits** from the **Data** pull-down menu and then typing either ON or OFF at the command line. These settings do not affect the actual limits of the screen but provide a check on whether you are staying within the limits as you draw. When you begin a new drawing, the limits are off and you can begin drawing an object with coordinates outside the limits. If the limits are on, you are prevented from drawing objects outside the limits. The warning

```
**Outside limits
```

is displayed. If you are consistently drawing outside the limits, you have probably set the wrong limits for your drawing and should resize the drawing limits accordingly.

Try It

- Change the Drawing Limits command and enter 24,12 for the upper-right corner.
- Zoom to view the drawing limits and then move the crosshairs to the upper-right corner of the screen to see the effects of the change.
- Change the upper limit to 6,4.5, initiate the zoom command again, and check the coordinates of the upper-right corner.
- Reset the upper limits to 12,9 and set the units to Engineering. Note that the coordinates of the upper-right corner are in inches.
- Reset the upper limit, this time typing 12',9'. Now check the coordinates again.

Reviewing the Coordinate System

Another important step to take before you begin entering data for a drawing is to review the coordinate system. AutoCAD uses the Cartesian coordinate system to keep track of the data that you supply.

The screen icon is located in the lower-left corner of the drawing area. With the default screen layout, the screen icon is hidden "behind" the Modify toolbar. To view this icon, point to the upper border of the Modify toolbar and drag the toolbar to the right. The screen icon shows the directions of the positive X (pointing to the right) and positive Y (pointing up) coordinate axes. Initially in this text you will be drawing two-dimensional objects, so the Z coordinates of all points will be zero. Chapter 6, in which you will draw three-dimensional objects, describes the screen icon and the Z axis in more detail.

As you begin to draw objects, you are prompted for the coordinates of various points. At that time you enter the X and Y coordinates for points in a drawing by typing the values on the command line or by picking the location on the screen with the mouse. If you know the exact coordinates of a point, you can enter them from the keyboard. However, if you do not know the exact coordinates, you have to use the mouse.

Angles are measured from the positive X axis. Positive angles are counterclockwise. This information is important when you use angles to describe the locations of points or when you rotate objects in the plane.

The coordinate system is illustrated in Figure 2-9.

Figure 2-9
Cartesian Coordinates

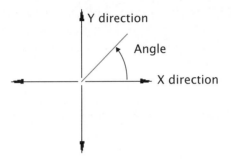

2-5   MANAGING YOUR FILES

To work successfully with AutoCAD, you need to master a few easy file-management skills. You must know how to save a file, open an existing file, and create a new drawing (the electronic equivalent of getting a fresh sheet of paper).

Saving a Drawing File

You should make a habit of routinely saving your drawings so you can retrieve them later and avoid the disaster of losing a large amount of work if the computer system goes down. Saving drawing files is a simple matter of specifying the name of the drawing and the drive or directory where the file is to be saved. To save a drawing, choose **Save** from the **File** pull-down menu. If this is the first time you have saved the drawing, the Save Drawing As dialog box shown in Figure 2-10 appears.

Figure 2-10
**Save Drawing As
Dialog Box**

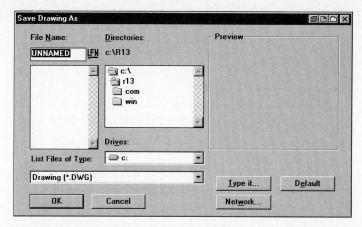

Type a file name in the File Name text box, and specify the drive and the directory for the file in the appropriate locations within this dialog box. You can choose the appropriate directory by double-clicking its name in the Directories list box. You can also change drives by clicking the down arrow to the right of the Drives list box and then clicking the drive you want. Click OK to complete the task and save your work. AutoCAD names your files and automatically supplies the .DWG extension. It is easy to open drawing files because by default AutoCAD displays the names of only the drawing files. If you want to save the file later without changing its name, choose **Save** from the **File** pull-down menu. If you want to save it under a new name, choose **Save As** from the **File** pull-down menu.

Try It

◆ Although you have not drawn anything yet, save your file as FIRST to save any settings you have changed. The file is saved to the default directory, which is probably C:\.

◆ Try saving your file to the A:\ directory. You need to have a formatted disk in drive A to do this.

Opening a File

Once you have saved a drawing file, you can open it later to resume your work. Choose **Open** from the **File** pull-down menu to open files that have been previously saved. The Select File dialog box shown in Figure 2-11 appears; as you can see it has many of the same list boxes and text boxes as the Save Drawing As dialog box.

Similar to the Save Drawing As dialog box, the directories on the current disk are listed in the Directories list box in the Select File dialog box. The current directory, which is most likely C:\, is where AutoCAD is searching for .DWG files. Any .DWG files in the current directory are listed in the File Name list box. (You can use the scroll bar to scroll up and down the list as needed.) To open a drawing file, click its name, and then click OK. To see the contents of one of the other directories, use the scroll bar as needed until the directory name is in view, and then double-click the name. The name of the current directory displayed at the top of the column changes, and the list of files also changes. If you can remember a

Figure 2-11
**Select File
Dialog Box**

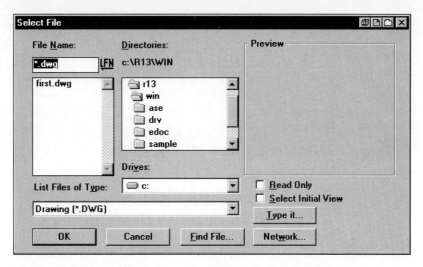

file's complete path and name (file name plus directory), you can type the name directly into the File Name text box and then click OK to open the file.

Try It

◆ Open the FIRST.DWG file in the C:\ directory.
◆ Try opening the file from the A:\ directory.

Creating a New Drawing

When you have completed a drawing, you may want to go directly to a new project instead of exiting AutoCAD. First you must clear the screen. You can do this by choosing **New** from the **File** pull-down menu. If you have not saved the current drawing, a dialog box appears asking if you would like to save your current drawing. You can choose from among three options: Yes, No, or Cancel. Select Yes if you want to save the latest changes to your current drawing. Select No if you do not want to save the version of the drawing on the screen. Select Cancel to continue with the current drawing.

Selecting either Yes or No opens the Create New Drawing dialog box shown in Figure 2-12. Type the name of the new drawing in the New Drawing Name text box, and AutoCAD clears the screen and puts the default settings of units and limits in effect. The other options in the Create New Drawing dialog box will be discussed in detail in Chapter 4.

Figure 2-12
**Create New Drawing
Dialog Box**

Try It

◆ Try creating a new drawing now, giving it a name of your choosing.

Exiting AutoCAD

When you have finished with a drawing session, you can exit the AutoCAD program by choosing **Exit** from the **File** pull-down menu. If you have not saved the current drawing file, you are asked about saving your current drawing. You can select Yes, No, or Cancel.

2-6   USING SIMPLE DRAWING TOOLS

Drawing with AutoCAD is a matter of drawing various geometric shapes on the screen (the drawing area) or editing existing shapes until the image you want is complete. This chapter demonstrates how to construct the easiest shapes: lines and circles. Drawing more complex shapes, such as arcs, ellipses, and polygons, is presented in Chapter 4. Most finished drawings are made up of some or all of these shapes. In this text, as in AutoCAD, the word *object* refers to a shape (a line, an arc, a circle, a box, a polygon, and so on) that has been drawn.

The task of editing objects is as important as drawing basic objects. Editing may include erasing all or part of an object, copying, moving, extending or trimming, and scaling or changing the size of an object. Later in this chapter you will learn some simple editing skills, and Chapters 3 and 4 present more editing techniques.

Drawing Lines

The most common objects in drawings are *lines.* Lines can be combined to construct other objects such as triangles and rectangles.

Initiate the Line command by clicking the Line button on the Draw toolbar. The Draw toolbar is shown in Figure 2-13 with all of the buttons labeled for you. Remember that if you forget which button you use to draw certain types of entities, you can merely point to the button and AutoCAD displays its function. If you hold down the left button on the mouse, the graphical pop-up menu shown in Figure 2-4 appears. Many times it is convenient to draw construction lines on a drawing. Construction lines help you make the drawing entities the correct size and they can be deleted later as needed.

Figure 2-13
Draw Toolbar

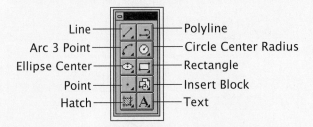

After selecting the line button, the following prompt appears in the command area:

From point:

Type the coordinates of the first point on the line, or pick a point on the screen by clicking with the mouse. AutoCAD supplies the next prompt:

To point:

Respond by typing the coordinates of the next point or picking the next point with the mouse. By default, AutoCAD draws continuous lines. This means that the end point for the first line becomes the start point for the second line. Thus, to draw the second line, you merely have to supply one endpoint for it. AutoCAD continues supplying the "To point:" prompt until you press (ENTER) without typing the coordinates of a point. If you move the mouse during the course of the command, you will see a line (called a rubber band) forming as the end of the line is dragged to a new position. This drag effect is common to many of the drawing commands.

Try It

- ◆ Change your drawing limits to 24,18 and zoom the drawing limits. Initiate the Line command and start drawing the square shown in Figure 2-14.
- ◆ Start the square at point 5,1.
- ◆ Enter 9,1 as the second corner of the square.
- ◆ Complete the square by entering the coordinates of the other corners.

Figure 2-14
Drawing Lines

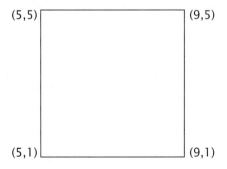

(5,6)

(5,5)　　　　(9,5)

(5,1)　　　　(9,1)

The Line command has a Close option for closing a figure of more than two sides—that is, drawing a line from the last selected point back to the first point. To issue the Close option, type C and press (ENTER) at the "To point:" prompt. For example, instead of entering the coordinates 5,1 to close the square, you could have entered the coordinates of the fourth corner 5,5, and then used the Close option to both complete the square and terminate the Line command.

Drawing Lines with Relative Coordinates

Sometimes you cannot enter coordinates simply as X,Y values. Consider, for example, drawing a rectangle when the length of the sides is not an integer. You could use the length of the sides to calculate the coordinates of the corners yourself. It is more convenient, however, to let the computer do the arithmetic for you with the use of *relative coordinates*. With relative coordinates you supply a change in X and a change in Y relative to the location of the last point that you entered.

After you enter the starting point to draw your figure, type the @ symbol followed by the change in X and Y of the next point. The @ symbol tells AutoCAD to add the following values to the coordinates of the previous point. For example, typing @3,2 tells AutoCAD to add 3 to the X coordinate and add 2 to the Y coordinate of the previous point.

Try It

Use relative coordinates to draw the upper rectangle in Figure 2-14. The horizontal sides are 3.2 units long and the vertical sides are 1.6 units long.

◆ Start the Line command again, and start the rectangle at point 5,6.
◆ Enter the relative coordinates in response to the "To point:" prompt.
◆ Complete the rectangle by closing it rather than repeating the initial coordinates. Save this drawing as RECT.DWG.

Another form of relative coordinates uses the *polar coordinate system*, in which the location of a point from the origin is calculated using the length of a radius (R) and the angle (α) the radius makes with the X axis. The horizontal and vertical distances between the origin of the polar coordinates and the second point are $R\cos(\alpha)$ and $R\sin(\alpha)$, respectively.

For example, suppose the distance between two points is 3.7, and the second point lies on a line that makes an angle α of 153 degrees with the X axis. You can locate the second point by entering @3.7<153, which means "Enter a point relative to the last point, 3.7 units along a line making an angle of 153 degrees with the positive X axis." When AutoCAD sees this entry, it computes the horizontal and vertical distances to the second point and adds them to the X and Y coordinates of the first point. This is much more convenient than having to do the arithmetic yourself. You can also use polar coordinates to draw orthogonally along angles of 0, 90, 180 and 270.

Try It

Draw the equilateral triangles shown in Figure 2-15 on your current drawing. Line AC is vertical, so line AB must be 30 degrees with the X axis. Since the internal angles of equilateral triangles are 60 degrees, line BC must make an angle of 150 degrees with the X axis.

Figure 2-15
Using Relative Polar Coordinates

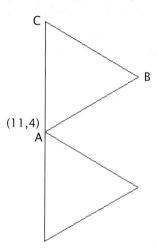

◆ Start the Line command, and start drawing your first line from the point 11,4.
◆ Type @3<30 and press (ENTER) in response to the first "To point:" prompt.
◆ Complete the triangle by entering relative polar coordinates for its remaining vertices.
◆ Draw the mirror image of the triangle about the X axis by substituting negative values for each of the angles in the last drawing.

Drawing Circles

Circles are another commonly used object in engineering drawings. A circle can represent anything from a hole through an object to a flange, a screw head, or the end of a pipe. The radius or diameter of a circle represents its size, while the coordinates of the center of the circle define its location. You can draw circles through two points that are the ends of the diameter, through three points (recall from geometry principles that three points uniquely define only one circle), or tangent to two other objects on the screen. To access the different methods for creating circles in AutoCAD, point to the Circle Center Radius button on the Draw toolbar and hold down the left button to open the graphical pop-up menu shown in Figure 2-16. A description of each of the options you can use to draw circles is listed in Table 2-2.

Figure 2-16
**Circle Graphical
Pop-up Menu**

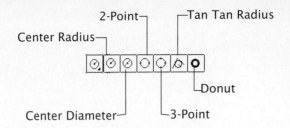

Table 2-2   Circle Options

Option	User's Response
Center, Radius	Enter the coordinates of the center point and the length of the radius.
Center, Diameter	Enter the coordinates of the center point and the length of the diameter.
2-Point	Enter the coordinates of points on the ends of the diameter.
3-Point	Enter the coordinates of any three points on the circle.
Tan Tan Radius	Select any two objects on the screen, and enter the length of the radius of the circle. AutoCAD constructs a circle that is tangent to the two objects and has that radius.

To draw a circle using the Center Radius option, select the appropriate button from the pop-up menu. At the prompt

        3P/2P/TTR/<Center point>:

pick any point on the screen, or enter the coordinates of the center point from the keyboard. At the next prompt

        Diameter/<Radius>:

enter a value for the radius, or move the crosshairs to select the radius. As you move the crosshairs, you see the circle forming. After you input the radius, the circle appears and the command terminates automatically.

The Center Diameter option is essentially the same as the Center Radius option. Select the appropriate button and enter the center point as before. The next prompt is

        Diameter/<Radius>: Diameter:

indicating that AutoCAD is expecting a value for the diameter. Enter the diameter from the keyboard or use the mouse to select the diameter. Again, as you move the mouse you see the circle forming. This time the position of the crosshairs is outside the circle as it forms.

To draw a circle with the 2-Point option, select the button from the pop-up menu. The prompt

        First point on diameter:

appears. Enter the endpoint of the diameter of the circle from the keyboard or by picking a point with the mouse. At the next prompt

```
Second point on diameter:
```

enter a second endpoint of the diameter to complete the circle. The circle forms as you move the crosshairs.

If you select 3-Point from the Circle graphical pop-up menu, the first prompt that appears is

```
First point:
```

Select a point on the circumference of the circle, and the next prompt

```
Second point:
```

appears. Select a second point. At the prompt

```
Third point:
```

select the third point on the circumference to complete the circle. The circle is formed as you move the crosshairs to locate the third point.

Try It

- ◆ Create a new drawing and name it CIRCLES.DWG.
- ◆ Draw a circle with its center at 7,6 and a radius of 1.5.
- ◆ Draw a circle with its center at 7,6 and a diameter of 1.5. These are the two concentric circles shown in Figure 2-17.
- ◆ Draw a two-point circle with the coordinates of the ends of the diameter at 4.5,4 and 5.75,3.5.
- ◆ Draw a three-point circle with points at 8.5,1.5, 7,2.4, and 8,4. Notice that the rubber band did not begin to form until you entered the first two points.
- ◆ All of these circles are shown in Figure 2-17.

Figure 2-17
Drawing Circles

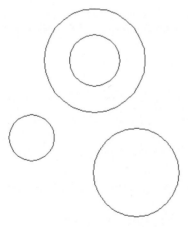

If you moved the mouse as you were creating the circles, you may have noticed that a circular rubber band was formed as the crosshairs moved. This is the same thing that happened when you moved the cursor during the Line command.

Drawing circles that are tangent to two other objects is more complex. You need to pick two objects and supply the radius. To pick an object on the screen, you move the crosshairs until the object goes through the pickbox and then press the left button on the mouse. Commonly, two different circles can be drawn tangent to two objects. AutoCAD calculates the location of the center of a new circle based on the radius and the two objects you selected. Which circle you get depends on where you pick the objects.

To draw a circle that is tangent to two objects in a drawing, select the Tan Tan Radius button on the Circle graphical pop-up menu. At the prompt

    Enter Tangent spec:

pick any object in the drawing using the pickbox. At the prompt

    Enter Second Tangent spec:

pick a different object in the drawing. At the prompt

    Radius:

enter a value from the keyboard. AutoCAD uses the value to construct a circle that is tangent to the two objects. If the circle cannot be constructed, the message

    Circle does not exist.

appears in the command area. This message usually means that the radius is too small.

Try It

- ◆ Create a new drawing and name it TTRCIR.
- ◆ Draw two lines from 6,7 to 10,2 and from 6,3 to 11,7.
- ◆ Select the Tan Tan Radius button.
- ◆ Pick the lines near their left ends as the first and second tangent specifications.
- ◆ Enter 1.5 as the radius.
- ◆ Repeat the task, selecting the lines near their right ends and using the same radius. Your screen should now resemble Figure 2-18. Notice that there is no rubber band because AutoCAD needs a specific radius before a circle can be completed.

2-7 USING SIMPLE EDITING TOOLS

This section presents some simple techniques for editing drawings. Before you can change objects in any way, however, you must learn how to select objects.

Figure 2-18
**Drawing Circles Using the
Tan Tan Radius Option**

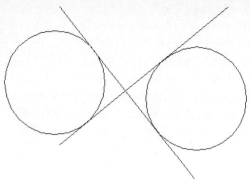

Selecting Objects for Editing

Much of your work in AutoCAD involves editing drawings—changing them to meet your changing needs or refining them to meet certain standards. To begin editing your drawings, you can first choose the editing command that you want to use and then select the objects you want changed, or you can select the objects and then choose the editing command. Both techniques are useful; it is up to you to decide which approach to use in any given situation.

Selecting Individual Objects   When you select the editing command first, the prompt displayed in the command area is

    Select objects:

The crosshairs disappear, but a small square—called an aperture— remains. You can select objects one at a time by moving the mouse until the object goes through the aperture and then pressing the left button on the mouse. When you select the object, it appears to be made up of short dashes, as shown in Figure 2-19. Two of the four lines making up the square in Figure 2-19 have been selected, and the aperture is visible on the right line in the square. AutoCAD responds by displaying the message

    1 found.

in the command area for each object selected.

Figure 2-19
**Selecting Individual
Objects for Editing**

Selecting Groups of Objects Using the aperture and selecting objects one at a time is not always the most efficient way to select a large number of objects at once. AutoCAD provides two types of windows you can use to select groups of objects: the Crossing (C) window and the Within (W) window. Using either of these window options means drawing a rectangle around the objects that you want to select.

When you use a W window, only those objects that are completely within the window are selected for editing. For example, the W window in Figure 2-20 selected only the left vertical line, because it is the only object entirely within the window. If you use a C window, all objects within the window and intersecting the boundaries of the window are selected. For instance, the C window in Figure 2-21 selected three lines: the two horizontal lines that intersect the window boundary and the left vertical line. One way that you can tell whether you are using a W window or a C window is that the W window has a solid border and the C window has a dashed border.

You start using windows by first choosing an editing command. Then you type either W (for within window) or C (for crossing window) and press (ENTER) at the

        Select objects:

prompt. AutoCAD prompts you for the

        First corner:

of the rectangle that will enclose the objects you want to select. You then use the mouse to select some convenient point on the screen. Next you are prompted for the

        Other corner:

which is on a diagonal of the rectangle from the first corner. As you move the mouse you can see the rectangular window being formed.

Figure 2-20
**Selecting Objects
with the W Window**

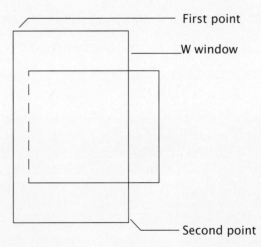

To indicate the type of window you want to use, you can choose the points of the window in a certain direction, instead of typing W or C at the prompt. When you pick the diagonal points for the rectangle from left to right, you create a W window. When you pick the diagonal points from right to left, you create a C window.

Figure 2-21
Selecting Objects with the C Window

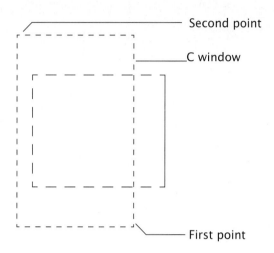

The third option for selecting groups of objects is useful when you want to continue editing the group used in the last editing command. AutoCAD remembers the last group of selected objects. If you respond to the

        Select objects:

prompt by typing P (for Previous) and pressing (ENTER), AutoCAD reselects the group of objects that was last selected and proceeds with the rest of the command. It should be noted that the Previous command does not work with the Erase command (to be discussed subsequently). Finally, if you respond by typing L (for Last) and pressing (ENTER), AutoCAD selects the last object that was drawn.

Selecting Objects Before Choosing an Editing Command To select an object before choosing the editing command, you use the pickbox. The selected object becomes dashed as before, and three small boxes appear on its ends and midpoint (or its center and radial points if it is a circle). These boxes, called grips, make certain editing commands easier to use. If you pick a point on the screen that is not on an object, you are prompted for the second corner. The second corner forms either a W or a C window depending on whether you move to the right or to the left from the initial point, and the appropriate objects are selected and equipped with grips. The grips in Figure 2-22 indicate which object has been selected. Once you have completed the selection process, you then select the editing command you want.

Figure 2-22
Selecting Objects Using Grips

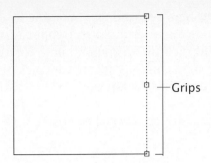

Using Erase and Undo

Erase is a commonly used editing command that does exactly what its name implies: It removes objects from a drawing. You can erase one or more objects with this command. If you change your mind, you can restore the erased objects with the Undo command. You initiate the Erase command by clicking the Erase button on the Modify toolbar (it is visible in the lower right corner of the toolbar as a pencil eraser). AutoCAD displays the prompt

        Select objects:

Select one or more objects by using any of the techniques described earlier. When you have finished selecting objects, press (ENTER) at the last

        Select objects:

prompt to complete the Erase command and delete the selected objects. Alternatively, you can first select the objects you wish to erase and then click the Erase button.

Using the Undo Command   You can recover erased objects by typing OOPS at the command line or by choosing **Undo** from the **Edit** pull-down menu. Only the last group of objects that were erased can be recovered.

Undoing Multiple Actions with the Undo Command

You can repeatedly choose **Undo** from the **Edit** pull-down menu to step backward through a series of commands you have issued. In other words, choosing Undo one time undoes the last command you issued, choosing Undo a second time undoes the command you issued previous to that, and so on. You can also use the Undo command to cancel several commands at once or mark groups of commands to be canceled. To use these advanced Undo commands, type undo at the command line. When you see the prompt

        Auto/Control/BEgin/End/Mark/Back/<number>:

you respond by typing A, C, BE, E, M, B, or a number and pressing ⒺⓃⓉⒺⓡ. The result of each response is listed in Table 2-3. The A (Auto) and C (Control) options are beyond the scope of this text.

Table 2-3   Undo Responses and Results

Response	Result
<number>	Represents the number of commands that you want undone. The default value is 1. If you enter any other number and press ⒺⓃⓉⒺⓡ, that number of commands will be undone.
M (Mark)	Places a mark in the sequence of commands. This option is useful if you want to experiment with some drawing steps before saving the results.
B (Back)	Undoes all of the commands back to the mark.
BE (BEgin) E (End)	Entering BE marks the beginning of a group of commands. Later entering E marks the end of the group. This group is treated as a single command when you issue the Undo command.

Using the Redo Command

The Redo command re-executes only the last command reversed by Undo. You initiate the command by choosing **Redo** from the **Edit** pull-down menu.

Try It

◆ Open the drawing file FIRST and click the Erase button.
◆ Select one of the lines in the small rectangle. Note the appearance of the line.
◆ Select another line in the small rectangle. Then complete the Erase command to erase the two lines.
◆ Use the Undo command to recover the objects you just erased.
◆ Erase some of the objects using a C window, and then restore them.
◆ Erase some of the objects using a W window. Note the difference between using these two options.
◆ Experiment with the use of the Redo command.
◆ Choose the Undo command several times to observe the results.

Figure 2-23
**Drawing Aids
Dialog Box**

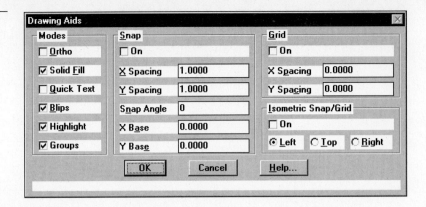

2-8   TAKING ADVANTAGE OF DRAWING AIDS

AutoCAD provides three drawing aids—Grid, Snap, and Ortho—that can assist you with the drawing process. Each feature helps you locate the position of the crosshairs quickly and with greater precision than is otherwise possible.

Using Grid

The Grid feature allows you to display a grid of dots on the screen. You can display or hide the grid by pressing (F7) or by double-clicking the Grid option on the status bar. You can set the horizontal and vertical distances between the grid points by using the Drawing Aids dialog box shown in Figure 2-23. To display this dialog box, choose **Drawing Aids** from the **Options** pull-down menu. The default value for each grid space is 0.0000. Change values by double-clicking on the X Spacing or Y Spacing box under Grid and then typing the new value. You can turn the grid on or off by filling in the On box. When you are satisfied with your settings, click OK. When Grid is on the message <Grid on> appears in the command area and the Grid option on the status bar appears in bold.

Using Snap

Closely associated with the Grid command is the Snap command. The Snap command sets up an invisible grid of points to which the crosshairs will snap when Snap is on. Press (F9) or double-click the Snap option on the status bar to turn Snap on or off. When Snap is on, the cursor will "jump" from one snap point to another on the screen. Thus, the snap points become the only pickable points on the screen. You set the Snap spacings by setting the appropriate values in the Drawing Aids dialog box, as shown in Figure 2-23. You can change the snap settings by double-clicking on the existing setting and typing in a new one. Setting the Grid and Snap points to some common interval can be a great help in laying out the basic outlines of a drawing.

When Snap is on, the message <Snap on> appears in the command area, and Snap appears in bold on the status bar.

Using Ortho

When Ortho is on you can draw lines only horizontally or vertically. Similarly, you can move or copy objects only in the horizontal or vertical direction. Turn Ortho on and off by pressing (F8) or by double-clicking the Ortho option on the status bar. You can also set this option in the Drawing Aids dialog box. When Ortho is on, the message <Ortho on> appears in the command area and Ortho appears in bold on the status bar.

Try It

◆ Move the crosshairs from the lower-left corner to the upper-right corner of the drawing area, and watch the coordinate display in the status bar.
◆ Turn on the Grid and Snap features, and note how the crosshairs jump as you move the mouse around slowly.
◆ Turn off the Snap feature, and note the smooth motion of the crosshairs.

Using Object Snap

The Snap drawing aid is useful when you are picking coordinate points that are on a regular rectangular pattern. However, you will often need to find a point that is established by one or more existing objects. For example, you may want to use the end of a line as the center of a circle. Or you may want to find the intersection of a line and a circle, or the intersection of two circles. In these cases you can use Object Snap (or Osnap) to help you locate points on the screen. In addition to finding intersections, AutoCAD can find midpoints and endpoints of objects, the centers of circles and arcs, points of tangency, and other types of points.

You can select an Object Snap mode by several different methods. You can choose **Toolbars** from the **Tools** pull-down menu and then pick **Object Snap** from the subsequent menu. The toolbar shown in Figure 2-24 appears. Another way to access Object Snap is by clicking the Object Snap button on the Standard toolbar (it looks like a dashed corner). If you have a three button mouse, you can access Object Snap by holding down the middle mouse button. Alternatively, you can type the abbreviation for the code words, referred to as Osnap modes, as described in Table 2-3. The abbreviation of each mode name is the capitalized part of the name. As you become familiar with AutoCAD, you will probably find it easier to type the Osnap mode rather than continuously returning to the menus to make your selection.

You enter an Osnap mode during the command sequence, when you would ordinarily enter a coordinate point. AutoCAD then prompts you with "of" or "to," depending on which Osnap mode and command you are

Figure 2-24
Object Snap Toolbar

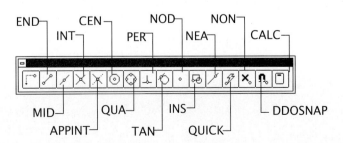

using. The "of" and "to" prompts tell you to select the object you want AutoCAD to find.

Table 2-3   Osnap Modes

Mode	Action
CENter	Picks centers of arcs and circles.
APParent INTersection	Picks the apparent intersection of two lines which do not actually intersect on the drawing.
ENDpoint	Picks the endpoint of objects nearest the end selected.
INSert	Picks insertion points of blocks and text.
INTersect	Picks intersections of objects.
MIDpoint	Picks midpoints of objects.
NEArest	Picks point on an object nearest to the crosshairs.
NODe	Picks a point object.
PERpend	Draws a line from the point perpendicular to the object.
QUAdrant	Picks the nearest cardinal point on an arc or circle. A cardinal point is the intersection of the X or Y axis and the object.
Quick	Allows AutoCAD to find the quickest point satisfying the Object Snap modes.
TANgent	Draws a line from the last point tangent to the object in the direction nearest the point selected.
NONE	Disables the current Osnap mode.

Try It

◆ Start a new drawing, and draw three circles similar to those in Figure 2-25.
◆ Start the Line command. At the "From point:" prompt type CEN and press (ENTER) to signal AutoCAD that you intend to use the center of a circle as the first point of the line. An aperture will replace the pickbox.
◆ At the "of" prompt use the aperture to pick any of the circles.
◆ Continue typing CEN after the "To point:" prompt until the three lines in Figure 2-25 are completed.

Figure 2-25
**Drawing Lines
with Object Snap**

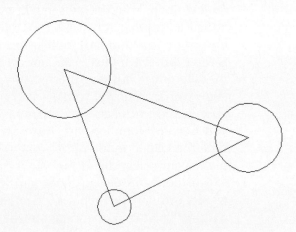

Figure 2-26
**Drawing Lines
and Circles with
Object Snap**

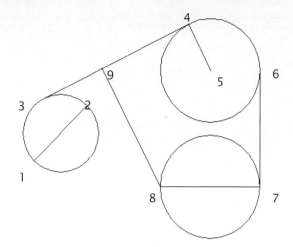

Try It

In this exercise you will draw several circles and a number of lines using various geometric points to be found by Osnap modes. The result is shown in Figure 2-26.

◆ Start a new drawing. Draw line 1–2 starting at 3.75,3.25. Make the line 1.50 units long at 45° with the X axis.
◆ Draw two circles, each with a radius of 1.0. Place the centers of the circles at 7.25,5 and 7.25,2.75.
◆ Draw the small circle with its center at the midpoint of line 1–2 with a radius equal to half the length of the line. Use the MID and END Osnap modes.
◆ Draw line 3–4 tangent to the small circle just drawn and to the upper large circle. Use the TAN Osnap mode twice.
◆ Draw a line 4–5 from the end of line 3–4 to the center of the upper large circle. Use the INT (or END) and CEN Osnap modes.
◆ Draw lines 6–7 and 7–8 using the QUA Osnap mode. Draw Line 8–9 using the END and PER Osnap modes.

Running Object Snap

In the previous section you had to enter the desired Osnap mode for each object that you drew. At times you will need to use the same Osnap mode repeatedly in a drawing, so you will want to keep the mode running while you draw. AutoCAD allows you to set one or more of the modes as running Osnap modes. After you have set the modes, AutoCAD uses them automatically without requiring you to type or select the codes individually.

To set running Osnap modes, choose **Running Object Snap** from the **Options** pull-down menu to display the dialog box shown in Figure 2-27. You can also click the DDOSNAP button on the Object Snap toolbar. To choose the modes you want to use, click the box to the left of the mode, and then click OK to close the dialog box. You can turn off the running Osnap modes by returning to this dialog box and clearing the boxes that you selected.

Figure 2-27
**Running Object Snap
Dialog Box**

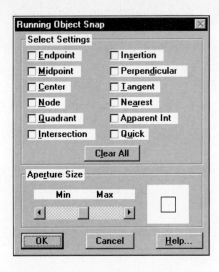

Using Aperture Size

When you select one of the Osnap modes, the pickbox changes into a much larger box called the aperture. You can control the aperture size by sliding the horizontal scroll bar under Aperture Size in the Running Object Snap dialog box. As you move the scroll bar, the size of the aperture changes. The box to the right of the scroll bar shows you the actual size of the aperture. If you have a very crowded drawing, the normal aperture may overlap more than one object. If so, you can reduce the size of the aperture to select objects accurately.

Try It

◆ Draw the large square and circle shown in Figure 2-28.
◆ Use running Osnap modes to draw the remaining lines in the drawing. Select the modes using the Running Object Snap dialog box.
◆ Increase the aperture to its maximum size, and observe the result.
◆ Return the aperture to an intermediate size.

Figure 2-28
**Running Object Snap
Exercise**

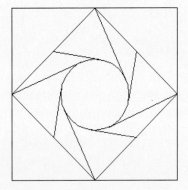

2-9   PLOTTING YOUR DRAWING

You can make copies of your drawings by plotting them with a pen plotter or by using your printer as a plotter. This discussion will be limited to plotting drawings with a printer. We will assume you have a printer attached to your computer and the correct driver (a software program) for your printer is installed so that it is available to AutoCAD. Normally you install the driver when you install AutoCAD. If you need help with the installation see the reference guides supplied with the AutoCAD program. If you are plotting your work in a lab environment, your lab assistant or instructor will be able to help you if you have any problems.

You must set the plotting parameters before you plot the drawing on a sheet of printer paper. You select what portion of the total drawing is to be plotted. In addition, you select the location, orientation, and size of the plotted image. AutoCAD provides you with the chance to preview the results of the selections before you send the plot to the printer.

Using the Plot Configuration Dialog Box

To plot your drawing, choose **Print** from the **File** pull-down menu. The Plot Configuration dialog box shown in Figure 2-29 is displayed.

Figure 2-29
**Plot Configuration
Dialog Box**

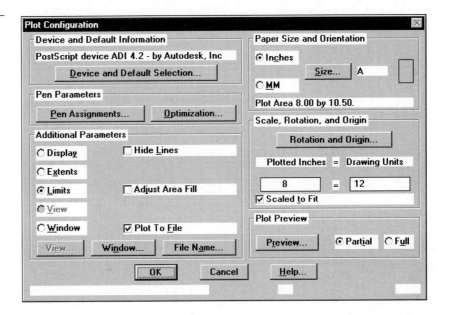

The dialog box is divided into six sections, each controlling a set of plotting parameters. Two sections, Device and Default Information and Pen Parameters, are beyond the scope of this discussion. The Additional Parameters section provides aids for selecting the portion of the drawing to be plotted. The Paper Size and Orientation section allows you to choose a paper size and units. You use the Scale, Rotation, and Origin section to set the ratio of the size of the actual object to the size of the drawn object, the orientation of the plot, and the location of the origin. After you choose these settings, you use the Plot Preview section to see the results of your choices before you actually send the drawing to the plotter.

Previewing a Plot   Before we discuss the selection of the plot parameters, it is useful to learn how to preview a plot using the parameters that have been preset by AutoCAD. Before sending a plot to the printer, you should preview the plot to see how each setting affects the results. The Plot Preview section gives you the choice of seeing only the outline of the effective plotting area or seeing the actual details of the drawing. Click the Partial button and then click Preview. The Preview Effective Plotting Area dialog box appears showing the outline of the paper, in red, and the outline of the drawing area, in blue. Information about the paper size and the effective area is shown in the box. AutoCAD checks the plot for potential problems. If any are found, a warning is shown in the Warnings box. Click OK to return to the Plot Configuration dialog box. If you want to preview the plot in detail, select Full before clicking Preview. A similar dialog box appears showing the actual drawing instead of the blue outline. You can examine the drawing more closely by using the Pan and Zoom option. This option is outside the scope of this text. If you are satisfied with the looks of the plot, click End Preview to return to the Plot Configuration dialog box.

Selecting the Paper Size and Orientation   This section is used to select the paper size and orientation of the plot and the units of measure, either inches or millimeters. The default units are inches, and this is the setting that you typically want to use. If you need to specify the paper size in millimeters, click MM. The orientation is fixed if you are using a printer as the plotting device. You will learn how to rotate the plot in a moment.

You must select the size of the paper you will use for the plot before you choose any of the other plot parameters. The outline that appears on the Preview Effective Plotting Area dialog box represents the standard paper size used with printers, approximately 8 by 10.5 inches. If you select Size in the Paper Size and Orientation section, the Paper Size dialog box appears. The settings in this dialog box depend on the actual plotting devices that are connected to the computer. The standard paper sizes in both inches and metric units are listed in the left column. You can also set customized paper sizes to be used with the printer by typing the dimensions in the Width and Height boxes on the right. These dimensions must be less than the maximum dimensions of the printer paper. You select the new paper size by highlighting the name in the left column and then clicking OK; this returns you to the Plot Configuration dialog box.

Setting Additional Parameters   The Additional Parameters section has five settings that determine how much of the drawing is included in the plot. One of these, View, will not be discussed here. The other four, Display, Extents, Limits, and Window, are used to select what portion of the drawing or screen is included in the plot. Display selects the current image on the drawing screen. Limits selects only that portion of the drawing within the Limits that you selected at the beginning of your drawing session. Extents selects the entire drawing, including objects currently off the screen. Window selects only that portion of the drawing within a window. You select any of the first three options by clicking the appropriate button. When you click Window the Window Selection dialog box appears.

You will construct a window similar to other selection windows you have used earlier in the text. You can select the coordinates of the corners of the selection window by typing new values in the First corner and Second corner boxes. It is easier, however, to select the window directly on the drawing screen. If you click the Pick box, the dialog box disappears and the prompt

First corner:

appears. Pick a point to define a window around the portion of the drawing to be plotted. At the

Second point:

prompt pick another point to complete the window. The Plot Configuration dialog box reappears and you can preview your selection.

Try It

- Make a simple drawing consisting of lines and circles.
- Initiate the Print command to display the Plot Configuration dialog box.
- If the Extents button in the Additional Parameters is not on, select it now.
- Preview the plot using the Partial option.
- Preview the plot using the Full option.
- Return to the Plot Configuration dialog box.
- Click Size to activate the Paper Size dialog box.
- Set the paper size at 5 by 5 inches.
- Select the new paper size and click OK.
- Preview the result.
- Reset the paper size to 8 by 10.5.

Setting Scale, Rotation, and Origin   The scale of the plot is the ratio of a plotted dimension to the actual dimension of the drawn object. For example, using a scale of 1/2 to plot a drawing means that a line with the length of 10 units in the drawing will be plotted to a length of 5 inches on the paper. This scale is defined as 1 inch equals 2 units, or 1=2. Commonly used scales are 1=2, 1=4, 1=5, 1=8, 1=10, and 1=100. You must calculate the scale to be used for your plot. The calculation is quite simple. First determine the maximum horizontal dimension of your drawing, including any text. Divide that number by the horizontal dimension of the paper. Repeat the step using the vertical dimension of the drawing and the paper. Use the larger of these two ratios as the scale, and select the standard scale nearest the calculated value.

The scale for the plot is set in the section on Scale, Rotation, and Origin. This scale is set by typing 1 in the Plotted Inches box and the related scale value in the Drawing Units box. If it is not important to use a precise scale for the plot, you can click the Scaled to Fit box (a check mark will appear in the box). AutoCAD automatically adjusts the settings to fit your drawing. Furthermore, the new settings will appear in the Plotted Inches and Drawing Units boxes.

You can change the orientation of the plot and control where the drawing origin coordinate point (0,0) is located on the paper. The default orientation is vertical, that is, the Y direction is vertical on the paper. The default location of the origin is near the lower-left corner of the paper. The remaining points in the drawing are plotted relative to that point on the paper.

Click the Rotation and Origin buttons and the Plot Rotation and Origin dialog box appears, offering four rotation settings, 0, 90, 180, and 270 degrees. Click the appropriate button to choose the rotation setting you want to use. You move the plot origin by typing a new value in the X Origin and Y Origin text boxes. Increasing the X value moves the image to the right on the paper, and increasing the Y value moves the image up the paper. Click the OK box to accept the changes and leave the dialog box.

Try It

- ◆ Set your drawing limits so that they are smaller than they were previously. Use the Zoom command to enlarge your drawing image so that it extends beyond the current screen area.
- ◆ Initiate the Print command.
- ◆ Click the Display button and do a full preview.
- ◆ Repeat the preview with the Limits button on.
- ◆ Click the Windows box and select a portion of the drawing to preview.
- ◆ Return to the drawing screen and do a zoom with the All option to restore the original drawing.
- ◆ Click the Scale to Fit box and note the scale settings, and then Preview the plot.
- ◆ Enter scale settings of Plotted Inches = 1 and Drawing Units = 5.
- ◆ Preview the plot.
- ◆ Enter scale settings of Plotted Inches = 5 and Drawing Units = 1.
- ◆ Preview the plot.
- ◆ Set the rotation angle to 90 degrees and use Full to preview the result.
- ◆ Move the origin 6 units to the right and 4 units upward, and preview the result.
- ◆ Place the origin at X = 0.5 and Y = 1.5, and preview the result.

Sending the Plot to the Printer   After you are satisfied with the plot parameters, click OK in the Plot Configuration dialog box. AutoCAD begins the plotting process, and various messages appear in the command area while plotting information is sent to the printer. If you need to interrupt the plot, type (CTRL)+C to cancel the process. The plot continues for a short time while the printer processes the information that is stored in its buffer.

Application 1   **CONNECTING PLATE**

Civil/Structural Engineering

The geodesic dome is used to shield people and equipment from the effects of the weather, wind, and earthquakes. The wind loads are transferred from the covering skin to the various rib elements. The ribs eventually transfer the loads to the foundation. All connections in a structural frame are extremely important to its safety. If only one of the connections in the structure fails, the entire structure can fail. The careful design of all connections is crucial to the integrity of the entire structure.

The drawing in Figure 2-30 shows the top and front views of a plate that is used to connect six ribs in the geodesic dome. The upper part of the figure shows the outline of the plate and the location of the ribs. The lower part of the figure shows the thickness of the plate and how the ribs are connected. In this application you will draw only the plate. The details of the bolt will be left for a later chapter.

You can use the five-step problem-solving process to draw the connecting plate.

Figure 2-30
Connecting Plate with Connecting Members

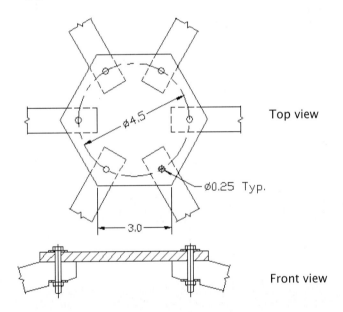

Top view

Front view

1. Identify the Object and Its Function

The object is a hexagonal plate that will connect six ribs in a geodesic dome.

2. Research Models and Determine Dimensions

The thickness of the plate is based on the loads the ribs will carry and the quality of the material used in the plate. The hexagonal shape of the plate is determined by the number of ribs that are to be connected. The structural engineer determines the dimensions by drawing on previous experience and similar designs that have been used. It is important to note, however, that every new situation is unique and, therefore, each design must satisfy the specific load conditions of the structure.

3. Make a Hand-drawn Sketch

You can use Figure 2-31 as the rough sketch. As you think about making the drawing, you have to decide on the order in which you will draw the lines and circles. In this project draw the polygon first. Then draw radial lines connecting the opposite vertices of the polygon. Next draw the circle around which the holes are located. Then, using the intersections of the radial lines and the circle as the centers, draw the small circles. Finally erase the extra lines and circle.

Figure 2-31
Connecting Plate

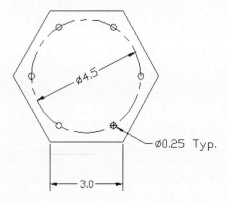

4. Make Appropriate Screen Adjustments

Set the units to Decimal with a decimal place tolerance of 2. This accuracy is consistent with the precision of the fabrication accuracy. Use the default limits.

5. Draw, Print or Plot, and Save the Drawing File

Use the Line and Circle commands to complete the drawing. When you have finished the drawing, save it as PLATE.

SUMMARY

This chapter introduced some of the basic features of AutoCAD. You gained some familiarity with the AutoCAD interface—the drawing screen, the menu systems, and various commands and dialog boxes. You also learned how to use on-line help. You discovered some of the essential steps you must take to set up your drawing, including selecting units and setting limits. You now know how to begin a new drawing, how to open an existing drawing, and how to save your drawing and exit AutoCAD. You learned the two most basic drawing commands: Line and Circle. You know how to select objects for editing and how to use the Erase, Undo, and Redo commands. In addition you learned about the Snap, Grid, and Ortho drawing aids. Finally, you learned how to configure and plot your drawing.

Key Words

aperture
cardinal point
Cartesian coordinate system
circle
click
command area
command line
crosshairs
dialog box
drawing area
function key
grid
grip
limit
line
menu bar

model space
mouse
object
Osnap mode
paper space
pickbox
polar coordinate system
pull-down menu
relative coordinates
scale
screen icon
status bar
text screen
title bar
toolbar

Exercises

Draw the objects in each of the following exercises. Do not attempt to reproduce the text or the dimensions.

Exercise 2-1
Column Base Plate

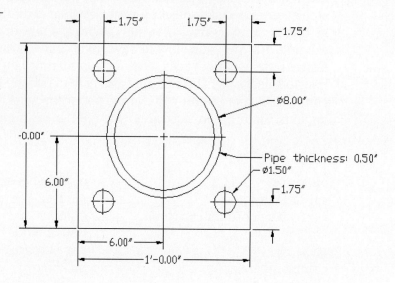

Exercise 2-2
Partial Site Plan

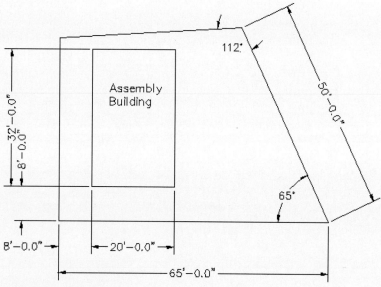

Units: Engineering
Limits: 0,0 to 80',60'

a. Draw the outline of the property boundaries.
b. Locate the lower-left corner of the building and draw the outline of the building.
c. Use the foot and inch symbols when you enter coordinates or distances.

Exercise 2-3A
Foundation Plan

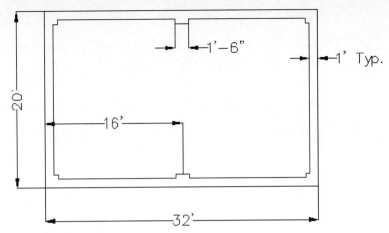

Units: Engineering
Limits: 0,0 to 36',27'

Exercise 2-3B
Corner Detail

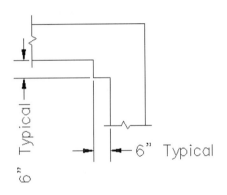

Exercise 2-4
Roof Framing Plan

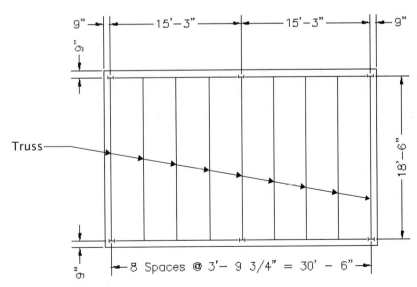

Units: Engineering
Limits: 0,0 to 36',27'

Exercise 2-5
Howe Roof Truss

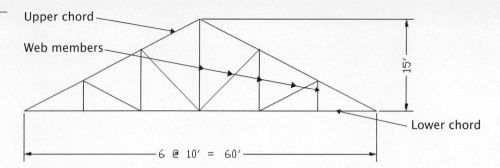

a. Draw the bottom chord as a series of 10-foot lines to provide endpoints for Object Snap.
b. Draw the upper chords next.
c. Turn on Ortho and draw the vertical lines from the lower chord to the upper chord using the END and NEArest Osnap modes.
d. Complete the drawing.

Exercise 2-6
Gusset Plate

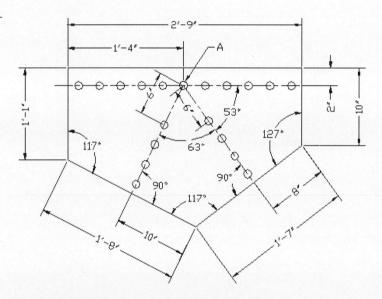

a. Draw the outline of the Gusset plate.
b. Draw the lines (starting at point A) through the holes as 3-inch segments to provide endpoints for Object Snap.
c. Use the END Osnap mode to locate the centers of the circles. The hole diameter is 1-inch.

Exercise 2-7
Base Plate Detail

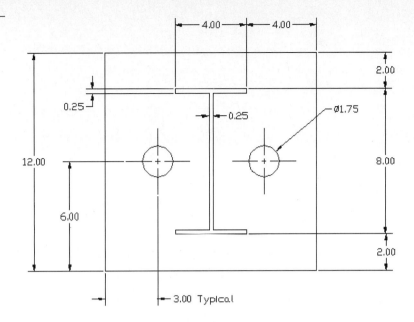

3 Learning Some Basic Editing Skills

Laser Technology $\;$ Since their discovery in the 1950s, lasers have been used to solve a wide range of problems—from medical to mechanical to musical. Surgical lasers remove cataracts, clear clogged arteries, remove brain tumors, and cauterize leaky blood vessels. Laser machine tools, controlled by computers, have increased the quality of manufactured products that require extensive and precise cutting of materials. Laser technology is also used to record and replay sounds and images. The quality of the sounds and images will not deteriorate with use because there is no physical contact between the recording and playing heads. At the end of this chapter, you will draw the schematic for an optical disk pick-up system.

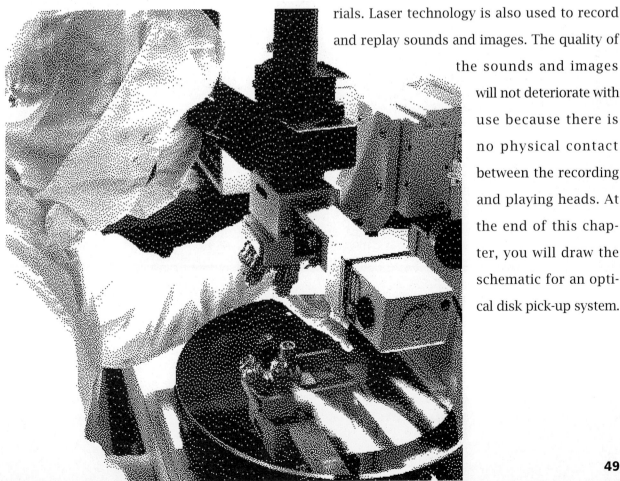

INTRODUCTION

You seldom complete a drawing by simply creating basic objects such as lines and circles. Usually, you need to use AutoCAD's editing features to refine the basic shapes in your drawing. So far you have used the Erase, Undo, and Redo commands. This chapter presents several additional editing commands. First you learn to use the Offset, Trim, Extend, Copy, Move, Mirror, and Rotate commands, which allow you to modify existing objects. Another command, Layer, helps you organize your drawing, placing different elements on different layers as well as changing the linetypes and colors of the objects. Finally, you learn how to clean up the screen with the Redraw command, create a close-up view of part of the drawing with the Zoom command, and see parts of the drawing that are outside the limits of the screen with the Pan command.

As you work through the Try It! exercises in this chapter, you will be creating the electrical circuit diagram shown in Figure 3-20. You should save your work at the end of each exercise so that you can come back to it at a later time if you are unable to finish the diagram in one session. In this chapter you will learn about most of the buttons on the Modify toolbar shown in Figure 3-1. You may need to refer back to this figure periodically as you work through the Try It! exercises in this chapter.

Figure 3-1
Modify Toolbar

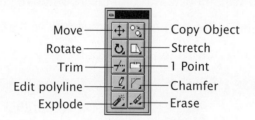

Move — Copy Object
Rotate — Stretch
Trim — 1 Point
Edit polyline — Chamfer
Explode — Erase

3-1   MODIFYING OBJECTS

When you begin to create more complex drawings, you will need a few new editing techniques to help you. Three of these techniques are the Offset, Trim, and Extend commands. You use Offset to draw lines which are parallel to one another or circles which are concentric with one another. You use Trim to trim away parts of objects that should not appear in the final drawing. In a similar way you use Extend to extend objects that are not complete. Using these commands is often easier than creating the correct image initially. Before we begin our discussion of Trim and Extend, however, you will first learn about the Offset command, since many times it is easier to trim or extend to an offset line or circle.

Using the Offset Command

You use Offset to produce a copy of an object (usually a line, circle, or arc) so it is *offset* from the original—that is, it is either parallel to or concentric with the original object. A copy of a line is exactly *parallel* to the original line and of the same length. A copy of a circle is a new circle with the same center as the original but with a larger or smaller diameter—that is, the two circles are *concentric*.

AutoCAD provides two methods for locating an offset copy. You can specify its distance away from the original, or you can specify a point through which the copy is to go.

Offsetting an Object by a Specified Distance   Figure 3-2 shows three lines that have been offset from a triangle by a specified distance. The Offset command copies each side of the triangle. Each line was copied to a location outside the triangle and at a given distance from the original lines. As you can see, the new lines are exactly the same length as the originals.

Figure 3-2
Offset Lines Created with the Distance Option

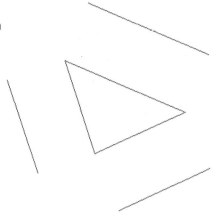

To start the Offset command, point to the Copy Object button on the Modify toolbar and hold down the left button on the mouse. Select Offset from the graphical pop-up menu that opens. AutoCAD displays the prompt

    Offset distance or Through <Through>:

If this is the first time you have used the Offset command in the current drawing session, type the distance that you want between the objects, and then press (ENTER). AutoCAD responds with the prompt

    Select object to offset:

Use the pickbox to select a single object. AutoCAD supplies the prompt

    Side to offset?

At this prompt, pick any point on the side of the original on which you want the copy to be placed. The copy is drawn, and AutoCAD redisplays the prompt

    Select object to offset:

You can pick another object (including the offset copy you just completed), or you can end the command by pressing (ENTER).

If you had used the Offset command previously during the drawing session, AutoCAD would have remembered the previous offset distance. For example, if you had specified 0.25 as the offset distance, the first offset prompt would be

        Offset distance or Through <0.25>:

You could have either accepted the value by pressing (ENTER) or entered a new distance.

    You can offset circles by specifying a distance in much the same way. The only difference is in the appearance of the result. A circle copied with Offset has a common center with the original but has a larger or smaller diameter. Figure 3-3 illustrates circles (one larger and one smaller) that have been copied using the Offset command.

Figure 3-3
Offsetting Circles

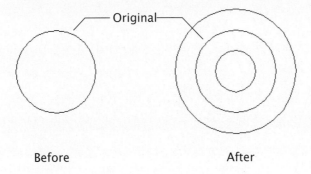

Before   After

Offsetting an Object Through a Particular Point   The Through option of the Offset command allows you to create a copy of the object that passes through a point of your choice. Using the Through option is a little different than using the Distance option, but the appearance of the result is the same for both options.

    As you know, choosing the Offset button from the Modify toolbar yields this prompt (note that if you have used the Offset command before, a default value may be displayed in the brackets instead of "Through"):

        Offset distance or Through <Through>:

Press (ENTER) to select the Through option if this is the default displayed in the bracket or type T and press (ENTER). AutoCAD displays the prompt

        Select object to offset:

After you select a single object to be offset, AutoCAD displays this prompt:

        Through point:

Pick a point on the screen (you may use any of the Object Snap options talked about in Section 2-7 to help you define a point on the screen), and the object is copied through that point.

Try It In this exercise you will begin to draw the objects you will need for the Ground and Capacitor symbols you will use in the electrical circuit diagram shown in Figure 3-20. When you finish this exercise, your drawing should look like the figure below. Note that many of the lines you will create in this exercise are construction lines, which you will delete or trim in the next Try It! exercise.

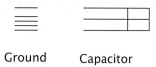

Ground   Capacitor

- Start up AutoCAD and create a new drawing. Set the drawing limits at 35,15. Draw two short horizontal lines on the screen. The length of the first line should be 1 and the length of the second line should be 3 (recall from Chapter 2 how to draw lines—you may wish to use relative coordinates to help you create these lines).
- Offset the shorter of the two horizontal lines you just drew a distance of 0.4 above the original.
- Offset the original shorter horizontal line a distance of 0.2 below it. When prompted to select the next object to offset, select the offset line you just drew and construct another offset line 0.2 below it. Repeat this procedure one more time. You should now have five shorter horizontal lines on the screen as shown in the figure above. The gap between the top and second line is 0.4 and the gap between the subsequent lines is 0.2.
- Offset the longer horizontal line twice, a distance of 0.5 above it and below it. Draw a vertical line at the right end of these from the end of the lower line and to the end of the upper line. Offset this vertical line 1.0 to the left.
- Choose **Redraw View** from the **View** pull-down menu to obtain a clear picture of your drawing. It should look similar to the one shown in the figure.

Using the Trim Command

You use Trim to erase parts of objects that extend beyond known boundaries. To carry out the command, you must first specify the boundary or boundaries and then select the ends of the objects to be trimmed. Figure 3-4 illustrates a typical situation where Trim is useful. In the final drawing the horizontal lines stop at the inclined line on the right. The task is to trim these lines back to the boundary. AutoCAD uses the term *cutting edge* to refer to the boundary. In Figure 3-4 only one cutting edge was used. However, the Trim command allows you to select as many cutting edges as you need for your editing project.

Figure 3-4
**Trimming Lines with
One Cutting Edge**

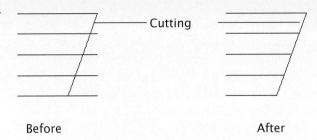

Before   After

To start the Trim command, click the Trim button on the Modify tool-bar. AutoCAD responds with the following prompt:

```
Select cutting edge(s)...
Select objects:
```

The first line of this prompt tells you that the objects you select at this time will be used to trim other objects. Use any selection technique to pick the cutting edges. Press (ENTER) when you complete the selection.

Next AutoCAD displays the prompt

```
<Select objects to trim>/Project/Edge/Undo:
```

Select objects one at a time using the aperture. The objects must extend beyond the cutting edge. The portion of the object that is trimmed depends on where you select the object. In Figure 3-4, for example, the right portions of the lines were trimmed because the lines were picked near the right ends. If the object to be trimmed does not intersect the cutting edge, AutoCAD displays the message

```
Entity does not intersect an edge.
```

and displays the prompt asking you to select objects. This prompt repeats until you press (ENTER) without selecting an object.

The example in Figure 3-4 involves trimming several lines to a single cutting edge. Sometimes you will want to remove a segment of a line between two cutting edges, as shown in Figure 3-5. The Before portion of the figure has two horizontal lines and two vertical cutting edges. The upper line is to be trimmed to the left cutting edge. The segment of the lower line between the two cutting edges is to be removed. The Trim command can perform both tasks easily.

Figure 3-5 illustrates two general rules about the Trim command:

- If the object to be trimmed is intersected by two or more cutting edges, and the object is not selected between a pair of cutting edges, the object will be trimmed to the nearest cutting edge. (This applies to the upper horizontal line in the figure which was selected towards its left end.)
- If the object is selected between cutting edges, the portion of the object between the cutting edges will be removed. (This applies to the lower horizontal line in the figure.)

Figure 3-5
**Trimming Lines with
Two Cutting Edges**

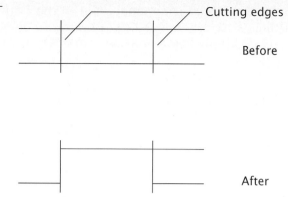

Trimming circles requires two cutting edges. The example in Figure 3-6 illustrates a common occurrence in engineering drawings. The object is closed on each end with semicircular arcs. The sides of the object are tangent to the arcs. In situations like this, you would draw the circles first. Then you would draw the lines tangent to the circles. You would finish the drawing by using the Trim command to remove the unwanted portions of the circle.

Figure 3-6
Trimming Circles

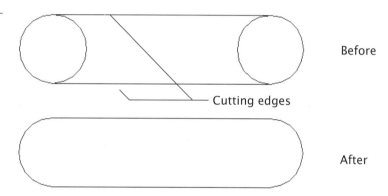

Using the Extend Command

The Extend command extends objects to selected boundaries. Figure 3-7 shows Extend being used to advantage. As you can see, the horizontal lines do not reach the inclined boundaries; you can use the Extend command to lengthen them so that they do.

Figure 3-7
Extending Lines to Lines

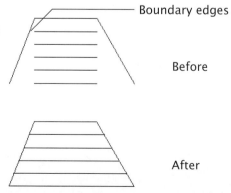

To issue the Extend command, point to the Trim button on the Modify toolbar, hold down the mouse's left button to open the graphical pop-up menu, and select the Extend button. AutoCAD displays the prompt

```
Select boundary edge(s)...
Select objects:
```

The first line of this prompt tells you that the objects you select at this time will be used as the boundaries for the extension of other objects. Pick the objects you want to use as *boundary edges*, and then press ⟨ENTER⟩. The next prompt is

```
<Select objects to extend>/Project/Edge/Undo:
```

Select the objects you want extended, making certain to pick the end of the object nearest to the boundary to which the object will be extended. If there are two or more boundaries, the object will be extended to the boundary nearest the point you selected on the object. If the object to be extended will not intersect any boundary, AutoCAD displays the message

```
Entity does not intersect an edge.
```

and repeats the prompt asking you to select objects. This prompt repeats until you press ⟨ENTER⟩ without selecting an object.

You can use circles as boundary edges with the Extend command. The circle can represent two boundary edges at once, as shown in Figure 3-8. If you select a circle as a boundary edge, the horizontal line can be extended to the left, and it meets the circle only once. However, the inclined line will, if fully extended, meet the circle twice.

Figure 3-8
Extending Lines to Circles

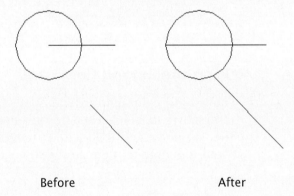

Before   After

Try It

In this exercise you will finish creating the ground and capacitor symbols for the electrical circuit diagram shown in Figure 3-20. Periodically you may have to choose **Redraw View** from the **View** pull-down menu to refresh the screen as you work. When you are finished, your drawing should look similar to the one shown in the following figure.

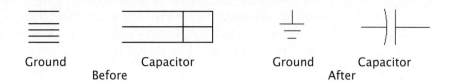

Ground   Capacitor   Ground   Capacitor

Before   After

◆ Draw a circle with a radius of 1.75 centered at the end of the middle longer horizontal line you drew in the previous Try It! exercise with a radius of 1.75. In the set of shorter horizontal lines that you created earlier, draw a vertical line from the midpoint of the uppermost line to the midpoint of the second line. Draw two more construction lines at this set of shorter horizontal lines. Each should start at the midpoint of the lowest line and should be drawn with relative polar coordinates. The first should have a length of 2 at an angle of 60 and the second should have a length of 2 at an angle of 120.

◆ Trim the three middle horizontal lines of the ground symbol to the angled lines just constructed (do not trim the top and bottom lines). If you make a mistake and trim away the wrong part of a line, choose **Undo** from the **Edit** pull-down menu to restore the line to its original state. Erase the top and bottom horizontal lines as well as the two angled lines. The ground symbol is now complete.

◆ For the capacitor symbol, trim the unnecessary portion of the circle away by selecting the upper and lower vertical lines as the cutting edges. Trim the middle portion of the middle horizontal line by selecting the arc and the offset vertical line as the cutting edges. Erase the upper and lower vertical construction lines as well as the right vertical line. Create an offset line and trim the left portion of the horizontal line so that the symbol looks proportionally correct (refer to the figure). The capacitor symbol is now complete.

3-2 DUPLICATING AND RELOCATING OBJECTS

AutoCAD offers several commands that make copies of objects. The Copy Object command can copy one or more objects, leaving the original intact and placing the copy in a designated location. You use the Move and Rotate commands to relocate one or more objects. Moving an object is much like copying it, except Move and Rotate delete the object from its original location. Like Copy Object, Mirror also makes copies of one or more objects. The Mirror command, however, makes a mirror image of the original object, while Copy Object makes an exact duplicate.

Copying Objects

To copy one or more objects to a specified location with the Copy Object command, you must select a *base point* on the object or group of objects. You can think of this point as the handle of the copy that will be carried to a new location. The base point is any convenient point, such as the center of a circle or the corner of a rectangle. Then you specify the new location of the base point, which determines where the new image will be located.

To issue the Copy Object command, click the Copy Object button on the Modify toolbar. The first prompt is

```
Select objects:
```

Select one or more objects using any of the selection techniques from Chapter 2. Complete the selection by pressing (ENTER), and this prompt appears:

```
<Base point or displacement>/Multiple:
```

To make a single copy of the selected object or objects, select the base point now (you can use any of the Osnap modes discussed in Chapter 2). You see the prompt

```
Second point of displacement:
```

Enter the new location of the base point. The command ends if you are making a single copy.

You can also use the Copy command to make multiple copies of one or more objects. Click the Copy Object button, as before, and select the object(s) you want copied. The prompt

```
<Base point or displacement>/Multiple:
```

provides the Multiple option. Type M and press (ENTER) to inform AutoCAD that you want to make multiple copies of the selected objects. AutoCAD responds with the prompt

```
Base point:
```

You supply a base point as before. AutoCAD continues to prompt you for the points of displacement until you press (ENTER) without entering a new point. A copy of the objects you selected will appear at each of the new points you have specified.

Moving Objects

You can use Move to move one or more objects to another location in the drawing. When you move a group of objects, all the objects are translated together—that is, each object you move maintains the same relative location with respect to the other objects. With the Move command, as with the Copy Object command, you select objects, select a base point, and specify the second point of the displacement. Unlike the Copy Object command, however, the Move command erases the original object(s).

To issue the Move command, click the Move button on the Modify toolbar. At the prompt

```
Select objects:
```

select the objects that you want to move. Again, use any of the selection techniques you learned in Chapter 2. The next prompt is

> Base point or displacement:

Pick a convenient point as the base point, just as you do for the Copy Object command. (Note that this prompt does not provide the Multiple option, because such an option does not make sense for moving objects.) At the next prompt,

> Second point of displacement:

pick the new location of the base point. The command terminates when you have picked the second point.

Mirroring Objects

The Mirror command is useful when the object you are drawing has one or more axes of symmetry. When symmetry exists you can draw one half or one quarter of the object and use the Mirror command to complete the drawing. The drawing in Figure 3-9 includes two axes of symmetry: the vertical and horizontal lines shown as dashed lines in the figure.

Figure 3-9
Mirror Example Showing Axes of Symmetry

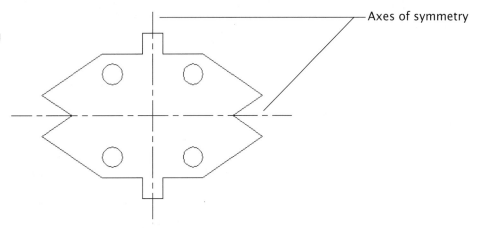

To initiate the Mirror command, point to the button on the Modify tool-bar. Click the Mirror button that appears on the graphical pop-up menu. AutoCAD displays the prompt

> Select objects:

After you select one or more objects and press (ENTER), AutoCAD presents the prompt

> First point of the mirror line:

Enter a point on the actual mirror line (again, you probably want to specify the points by using one of the Osnap modes). If the mirror line is not a part of the drawing, select a point on an imaginary line that represents the axis of symmetry. Next AutoCAD displays the prompt

Second point:

Enter any other point on the mirror line. Finally AutoCAD shows the prompt

Delete old objects? <N>.

Now you can delete or retain the old image—that is, the object(s) you selected initially. If you press (ENTER), the original objects are retained. If you type Y and press (ENTER), the old objects are deleted, and the resulting image is a mirrored copy of the original. In most engineering drawings you will not delete the old objects.

Your mirror lines need not all be vertical or horizontal. Figure 3-10 illustrates the result of using an inclined mirror line. The points on the original image and the corresponding points on the mirrored copy are equidistant from the mirror line. For example, the two points marked A represent a pair of corresponding points.

Figure 3-10
Inclined Mirror Line

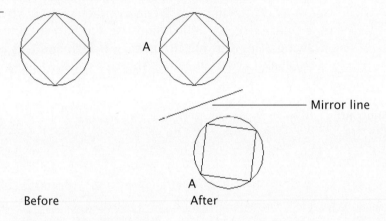

Rotating Objects

The Rotate command rotates objects about a specified point. Rotating an object involves three steps: First you select the object or objects to be rotated. Second you select the proper point for the center of rotation. Third you determine the amount of rotation.

The drawing in Figure 3-11 shows an object in an incorrect position and the same object rotated so that it is in the correct position. In this example the object is rotated 90 degrees clockwise, with the lower right corner as the center of rotation.

Figure 3-11
Rotate Example Using Rotation Angle Option

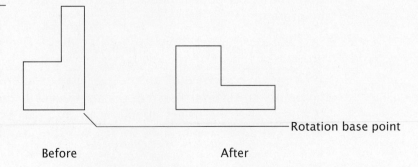

Start the Rotate command by clicking the Rotate button on the Modify toolbar. At the prompt

```
Select objects:
```

select the objects to be rotated by using any selection technique. At the prompt

```
Base point:
```

pick an appropriate point. The next prompt

```
<Rotation angle>/Reference:
```

gives you two ways to enter the rotation. Entering an angle and pressing (ENTER) automatically selects the Rotation Angle option and completes the command. A positive angle causes a counterclockwise rotation, and a negative angle causes a clockwise rotation. Alternatively, you can merely drag the objects to their desired new rotation and click when the rotation is correct.

On occasion you may need to rotate an object without knowing the precise angle of rotation. If this is the case, type R (for Reference) and press (ENTER) at the prompt

```
<Rotation angle>/Reference:
```

In the exercise shown in Figure 3-12, for example, the problem is to rotate the arc so its two endpoints are on the horizontal line. In this case you do not know the angle of rotation (labeled "Reference angle" in the figure). If you know the current orientation of some line, real or imaginary, and you know the new orientation, you enter the two angles at the prompts

```
Reference angle <0>:
```

and

```
New angle:
```

AutoCAD uses the difference between the angles to compute the rotation angle.

Alternatively, you can respond to the prompt

```
Reference angle <0>:
```

by picking a point, usually the base point, as the first point in the reference direction. AutoCAD then prompts you for a

```
Second point:
```

Pick a second point along a line in the reference direction. AutoCAD uses the second point with the first point to establish the reference direction (see Figure 3-12). Now you must establish the new orientation the reference direction is to take. At the prompt

    New angle:

pick another point along a real or imaginary line through the base point to establish the new direction (see Figure 3-12). AutoCAD calculates the angle between the two directions and uses the result as the rotation angle.

Figure 3-12
Rotate Exercise Using the Reference Option

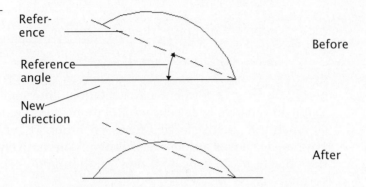

Try It

In this exercise you will create the final two symbols (resistor and transistor) you will need to complete the electrical circuit diagram shown in Figure 3-20. You will then work on the diagram so that it looks like the one shown in the figure below.

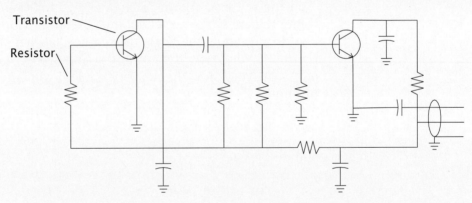

◆ To create the transistor, first start by drawing a circle with a radius of 0.9 away from your other symbols you have created. Draw a horizontal line from the center of the circle to a radial point on the left of the circle. Draw a vertical line from the midpoint of the line just created to a point 0.6 above this midpoint. Draw an angled line from the midpoint of this vertical line, which has a length of 2, at an angle of 30. Trim this angled line back to the circle.
◆ Mirror the vertical and angled lines about the horizontal line you first constructed. Make sure you keep the old objects when executing the mirror command. Trim the horizontal line from the circle center back to the vertical line.
◆ Draw an arrowhead at the end of the lower angled line by first drawing one small line and then mirroring this small line about the angled line.

Your transistor symbol is now complete.

◆ The resistor symbol will be drawn as a polyline. In AutoCAD, a polyline is a series of connected lines or arcs that are treated as a single object. Turn the Grid and Snap drawing aids on, and set the spacing of each to 0.2. Select the Polyline button on the Draw toolbar and draw the resistor symbol from grid point to grid point so that it looks proportionally correct relative to the other symbols you have on your drawing.

◆ Reset the Snap and Grid spacing to 0.5, and then zoom the drawing limits. Draw the necessary lines to construct the outine of the circuit as shown in the figure. After completing the outline, copy, move, and rotate the various symbols as needed on your drawing. As you draw remember all of the other commands you have learned about (Trim, Extend, Redraw View, and so on). You will probably have to turn Snap on and off repeatedly as you draw.

3-3 MANAGING YOUR WORK SPACE

You can also fine-tune your drawings by organizing them more carefully. This section explains how to use layers to separate different features of your drawing, as well as how to apply different linetypes and colors and how to move to the various layers of your drawings.

Working With Layers

So far you have been drawing on a single layer, but with AutoCAD you can actually draw on many different layers. AutoCAD layers are similar to transparent overlays. Imagine a set of drawings used to build a house. The drawings show the foundations on one sheet, the electrical wiring on another, the plumbing on still another. In addition, the structural framing for the different floors and roof are drawn on their own sheets. With AutoCAD, instead of creating separate drawings, you can represent these various sheets as separate layers in a single drawing. Layers enable you to work with different components of your drawing separately, and also to view them together.

You can set up different layers, name them, and assign certain types of information to each. Then you can turn the layers on or off at will to reveal or conceal the information they contain. When you have finished the project, you can display the layers in any combination for printing.

You change the appearance of lines, called linetypes, as well as the color of lines on specified layers. For example, some drawings may include details that are not on the outside surface of the object but are hidden. In this situation you can use the Hidden linetype. Likewise, when a drawing includes many layers, it is helpful to assign a different color to each.

Although you can display many layers at a time, you can only draw on a single layer. The layer that you are working on is the current layer. So far you have been drawing only on AutoCAD's default layer, which is called Layer 0. The name of the current layer is displayed on the left in the Layer Control box of the Object Properties toolbar. Graphical options that are set for the layer are also shown in this box. For example, a padlock is shown in an open position if the particular layer is "unlocked" and is shown as a closed padlock if the layer is "locked." The other options found on the Object Properties toolbar are used to set and control layers. The default linetype assigned to Layer 0 is Continuous.

You can create layers, assign linetypes and colors, turn layers on or off, and more by using the Layer Control dialog box shown in Figure 3-13. To display this dialog box, choose **Layers** from the **Data** pull-down menu. This dialog box displays all of the layers in a drawing and allows you to make several changes at once. As you can see in Figure 3-13, the current drawing includes two layers, Circles and Lines, in addition to Layer 0. The first time you activate the dialog box, it lists only Layer 0.

Figure 3-13
**Layer Control
Dialog Box**

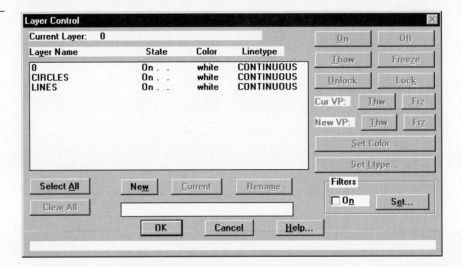

You must create new layers before you can change any of the features, such as linetype or color. To add a layer, first type its name in the blank box just below the New button in the Layer Control dialog box. Then click the New button, and the name of the layer is added to the list of layers.

Loading and Changing Linetypes So far your drawings have consisted of continuous (solid) lines. You usually use continuous lines to outline the visible details of the device. You can also use different linetypes to represent other information. Hidden and Center are two of the most common linetypes. Hidden lines consist of a series of short dashes separated by short spaces. You use Hidden lines to indicate that the feature of the device is an interior, or hidden, feature. Center lines are a series of long dashes alternating with short dashes. You can use them to makr the centers of circles.

You can assign AutoCAD's standard linetypes to layers or to specific objects in a drawing. First, however, you must load the linetypes. Choosing **Linetype** from the **Data** pull-down menu opens the Select Linetype dialog box shown in Figure 3-14.

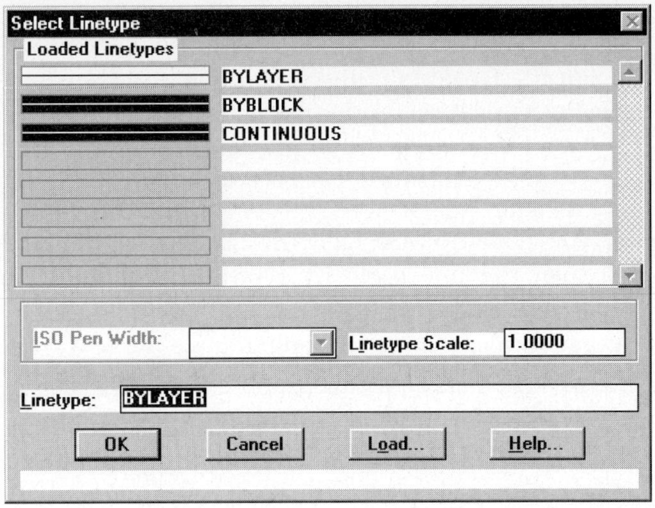

Figure 3-14
**Select Linetype File
Dialog Box**

When you click Load from the Select Linetype dialog box. another dialog box appears displaying the various linetypes AutoCAD offers. Figure 3-15 shows a partial list of the standard AutoCAD linetypes. You can either select the linetypes you wish to load individually or click Select All and then OK in this new dialog box to make the specified linetypes available in your drawing.

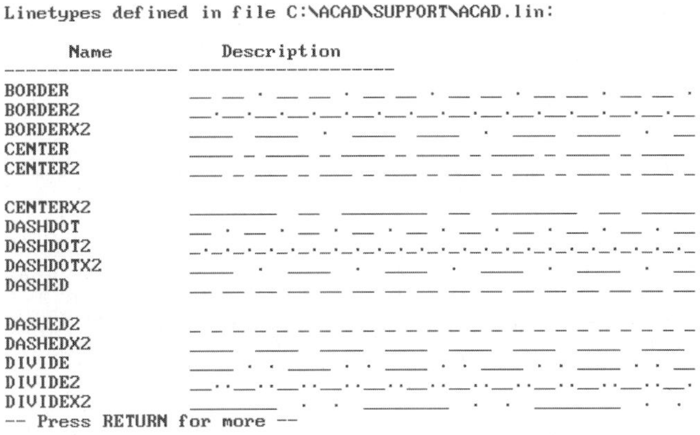

Figure 3-15
Standard Linetypes

To change the linetype for a layer, first activate the Layer Control dialog box. Select the layer you want to modify by clicking its name; it will become highlighted. Next click Set Ltype to display the Select Linetype dialog box. Scroll through the list to see all of the possible linetypes. To assign a linetype to the layer, click the linetype, and then click OK in the Select Linetype dialog box and in the Set Ltype dialog box.

Changing the Line Scale   AutoCAD allows you to change the length of the spaces between the dashes or dots in a selected linetype. This is particularly useful if you are making large-scale drawings. For example, say you were drawing a building that is 100 feet by 150 feet. If you draw a dashed line on the building, the default dash length of 1/8 inch would appear as a continuous line when plotted or displayed. You can change the line scale of all of the lines on the drawing or just of individual lines.

In general, you will probably want to change the line scale of all of the lines or the global line scale. To change the line scale, choose **Linetypes** from the **Options** pull-down menu and then select **Global Linetype Scale** from the next menu that appears. AutoCAD displays the prompt

        New scale factor <Default value>:

If you have not changed the line scale, the default value is 1.0. You can change the line scale by typing a new value, at which point AutoCAD regenerates the drawing database and applies the new scale to all previously drawn objects. Typing a value less than 1.0 results in smaller dashes, and typing a number greater than 1.0 results in larger dashes. Typically you want to set your line scale to the reciprocal of the scale to which you will be plotting your drawing. For example, if you plan on plotting the drawing at a scale of 1/4"=1'-0" (a 1:48 scale), then you should set your line scale to 48.

   Figure 3-16 illustrates the effect of different line scales on the same objects. The rectangle on the left was drawn using the Center linetype with a line scale equal to 0.5. The rectangle on the right is drawn with a line scale equal to 1.0. As you can see, the smaller the line scale, the shorter the individual line segments that make up the linetype.

Figure 3-16
Comparing Line Scales

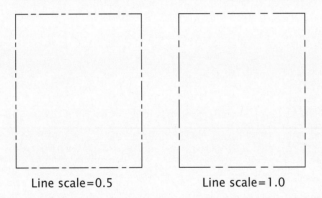

Line scale=0.5   Line scale=1.0

Choosing New Colors   You can assign colors as well as linetypes to various layers. First you open the Layer Control dialog box and select the layer you want to apply color to. Select Set Color, and the Select Color dialog box shown in Figure 3-17 appears. This dialog box includes a full palette of the colors AutoCAD offers. (The actual colors are not shown, but the layout of the box is clear.) Normally you will use one of the nine standard colors displayed across the top of the dialog box. You select a color by clicking the appropriate box. Colors are useful to help distinguish between different features and layers when more than one layer is on.

Figure 3-17
Select Color Dialog Box

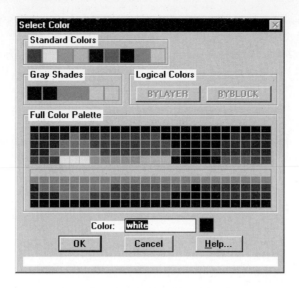

Changing the Properties of an Object

You can change the properties of objects in your drawing—including their color, layer, linetype, and thickness. The thickness property is associated with three-dimensional objects and will be discussed in Chapter 6.

To change the properties of objects on your drawing, choose **Properties** from the **Edit** pull-down menu. The following prompt appears:

```
Select objects:
```

Select the objects to be changed, and then press (ENTER). Depending on the number of objects that you have selected, different dialog boxes will appear. If you have selected only one line, the Modify Line dialog box shown in Figure 3-18 appears. If you have selected a single circle, the Modify Circle dialog box appears (it is very similar to the Modify Line dialog box).

Select the property you want to change (color, layer, or linetype) by clicking the appropriate button. Change the line scale for just the selected object by entering a new scale factor in the Linetype Scale text box. Alter-

Figure 3-18
Modify Line Dialog Box

Modify Line

Properties

Color...	BYLAYER	Handle:	28
Layer...	0	Thickness:	0.0000
Linetype...	BYLAYER	Linetype Scale:	1.0000

From Point
Pick Point <
X: 11.73181833
Y: 6.163117759
Z: 0.0000

To Point
Pick Point <
X: 19.27192999
Y: 9.430312751
Z: 0.0000

Delta XYZ:
X: 7.5401
Y: 3.2672
Z: 0.0000

Length: 8.2175
Angle: 23

OK   Cancel   Help...

natively, you can change the points that define the line in the text boxes labeled From Point and To Point within the dialog box. For each property you choose to change, a new dialog box appears. Select the new property, and click OK to return to the original dialog box. When you complete the changes, click OK. The dialog box disappears, and the object is displayed with its new properties.

If you want to change the properties of more than one object, the Change Properties dialog box appears after you select the objects. This dialog box is similar to the one shown in Figure 3-18 except that only the Color, Layer, Linetype, Linetype Scale, and Thickness options are available.

Adding Simple Text to Your Drawing

Usually your drawings will not merely consist of lines, circles, and other objects. You will have to add annotation to your drawings in the form of dimensions and notes. Notes are added as text to your drawings. You will learn about some of the more advanced methods for adding text to your drawings and about adding dimensions to your drawings in Chapter 5.

To add text to a drawing, click the Text button on the Draw toolbar. AutoCAD displays the following prompt:

Attach/Rotation/Style/Height/Direction/<Insertion Point>:

To select the location of the text on the drawing, you create a window around the area where the text is to be located. After you have specified the text location, the Edit MText dialog box shown in Figure 3-19 appears.

Figure 3-19
Edit MText Dialog Box

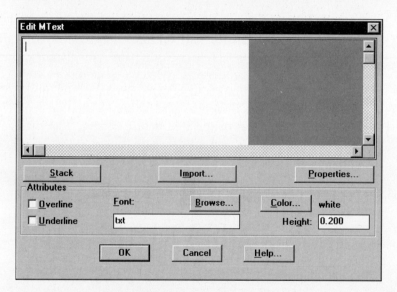

The upper half of the dialog box is a large text box, in which you type the text you want to appear on your drawing. If you wish to change the properties of the text, click Properties. The MText Properties dialog box appears that allows you to change the text height and style as well as other properties. Select OK in both dialog boxes and the text will be displayed on your drawing at the location you specified.

Try It When you are finished with this exercise, your drawing should look similar to the one shown in Figure 3-20.

Figure 3-20
Electrical Circuit Diagram

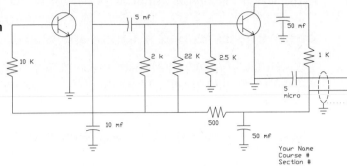

◆ Add three new layers to your drawing called Hidden, Text and Symbols.

◆ Load the linetypes into your drawing and then set the linetype for the Hidden layer to Hidden.

◆ Switch to the Hidden layer and draw the dashed ellipse shown in the figure on the lower right. (NOTE: To draw the ellipse, select the Ellipse button from the Draw toolbar, and then select the center point and a radial point on the short axis of the ellipse. Drag the vertical axis until the ellipse is the correct approximate size and click.) You may wish to draw the ellipse off to the side on your drawing and then move and/or rotate it to place it properly in your drawing.

◆ Switch to the Text layer, and add the necessary text to your drawing, making sure you insert your name and course information on the drawing. When you add the text, change the properties so that the text height is 0.3 instead of 0.2.

◆ Move the objects that make up the symbols on your drawing so that they are on the layer called Symbols.

◆ Change the properties of the horizontal line below the ellipse to make it dotted as shown in Figure 3-20.

◆ Experiment with displaying just one, two or three layers of your drawing at a time. Obtain a plot with shows just the Symbol layer and Layer 0. Obtain another printout that shows all of the layers.

3-4 CHANGING THE SCREEN DISPLAY

A number of AutoCAD commands allow you to control what is displayed on the screen. The most useful display commands, for the beginner, are Redraw, Zoom, and Pan.

Redrawing the Screen

The Redraw command removes the blips on the screen that accumulate as you draw and edit objects. You have already used this command in working some of the Try It! exercises in this text. Also, some editing commands cause part or all of an object to disappear. For example, if an object is entirely or partially behind another object that you erased, it appears to disappear. Redraw restores the image.

To initiate the Redraw command either type REDRAW in the command area, and then press (ENTER) or choose **Redraw** from the **View** pull-down menu. The screen is redrawn or refreshed. It is good practice to use Redraw periodically as you draw.

Zooming in to Get a Close-up View

The Zoom command allows you to *zoom* in on, or enlarge, part of a drawing (you can also zoom out to make the drawing appear smaller). Some drawings have so much detail that it is difficult to select objects and points for editing. In such cases, you can zoom in on a section of the drawing to magnify it. The Zoom command does not change the actual size of objects; rather it changes your view of them. This is analogous to your view of a house from an airplane compared to when you are standing right next to it. The size of the house doesn't changed, but when you are close to it, it appears large and when you are far away from it, it appears small. (To change the size of objects in a drawing, you use the Scale command, which is discussed in Chapter 4.)

Choose **Zoom** from the **View** pull-down menu to see the entire set of options that you can use with the command. You can also type ZOOM in the command area, press (ENTER), and then type the first letter of the option you wish to execute. As with other AutoCAD commands, after you get used to typing the command in you may find it faster than going through the menu structure. Some of the commands found on the Zoom menu are not available if you activate the Zoom command from the Command Line. Each Zoom option and result is described in Table 3-2.

The Zoom command is transparent, which means that you can use it from the **View** pull-down menu while another command is in progress. The current command will be temporarily suspended while you complete the zoom operation.

The All option is one of the three most useful Zoom options. When you work on a complicated drawing, parts of the drawing may disappear from view. You can use the All option to bring the entire drawing back into view. Occasionally you "lose" an object by moving or copying it to some remote location off the screen. You can use the All option to locate the "lost" object and erase it if necessary.

Window is another useful Zoom option. In a particularly crowded drawing it may be impossible to pick out a detail that you need for editing. For example, you may be trying to see the intersection of two objects to use with the INT Osnap mode. You can enlarge the detail around the intersection using the Window option.

When you initiate the Window option, AutoCAD displays the following prompt:

    First corner:

Pick the first corner of a window that contains the detail you want to enlarge. At the

    Other corner:

Table 3-2 Zoom Options and Results

Options	Result
In	Zooms in by a factor of two.
Out	Zooms out by a factor of one-half.
A (All)	Displays the area of the drawing defined by the limits or extents, whichever is greater. The extents define the area actually occupied by any part of a drawing.
C (Center)	Displays a view based on a point you select as the center of the screen after Zoom is executed. You are prompted for a magnification factor or a height. If you enter a numerical value, it is interpreted as the height in the drawing units being used. A value followed by an X (for example, 5X) is interpreted as a magnification factor.
D (Dynamic)	This option is too complex to be useful at this time.
Limits	Zooms to the drawing limits you have set.
E (Extents)	Displays the entire drawing, forcing it to the left area of the screen. This option is useful when looking for objects that disappeared from view during an editing command such as Copy or Move.
L (Left)	Displays a view based on a point you pick as the lower-left corner of the new display.
P (Previous)	Restores the previous display created by the Zoom command in the current editing session. AutoCAD remembers the zoom sequences so you can back up through the displays. If you back up through all of the zooms, AutoCAD displays the message "No previous view saved."
V (Vmax)	Creates the largest view that does not require regeneration.
W (Window)	Enlarges a rectangular area to the size of the screen area. You are prompted to enter a first corner and the other corner.
Scale(X/XP)	This is the default option. Enlarges or reduces the drawing display. If you enter a numerical value followed by an X (for example, 5X), the factor applies to the current display. A factor without the X applies to the area defined by the limits of the drawing. The XP suffix applies to paper space units and is beyond the scope of this module.

prompt, pick a point on the opposite (diagonal) corner. Now the section of the drawing in the window is enlarged. The center of the window is the center of the screen. Unless you choose a rectangle that is in proportion to the screen dimensions, objects outside the window may also be displayed.

Figure 3-21
Using the Window Option of the Zoom Command (Before)

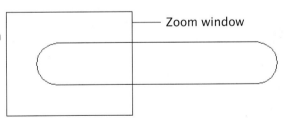

Zoom window

Before

Application 1   OPTICAL DISK PICKUP SYSTEM

Optical Engineering

A laser disk is similar to a conventional recording disk. The grooves form a spiral curve. The information on a conventional disk is stored as physical deformations in the shape of the groove. The information is played back by running a pickup needle through the groove. Eventually the deformations wear out and the recording deteriorates. The information on laser disks is also stored as deformations, but the deformations are formed by high-powered lasers. The data on the disk is in the form of binary code—a series of 0s and 1s. The information is read by a low-powered laser beam from a laser diode. The laser diode is focused with a lens, and the reflected light is, in turn, focused on a detector. Finally the data is sent to an electronic device, called an *optical disk pickup system*, for conversion to sound or graphic images.

1. Identify the Object and Its Function

The object is the schematic of an optical disk pickup system typically used for audio and video optical disks. The system is designed to read the data recorded on a special optical disk.

2. Research Models and Determine Dimensions

There are several optical disk pickup systems on the market today. You will find basic information about these systems in textbooks on optical systems. The system shown in Figure 3-25 represents a typical design. Since you will be drawing a schematic, or diagram, of the system, dimensions are not necessary. Draw the size of the individual objects so that the elements are proportional to one another.

3. Make a Hand-drawn Sketch

Use Figure 3-25 as the rough sketch. Plan the location of the components so that they line up properly. You will probably do best if you draw the lenses first.

4. Make Appropriate Screen Adjustments

Use New to start the drawing. Save the drawing as OPTICAL.

5. Draw, Print or Plot, and Save the Drawing File

Draw the schematic as shown. The lenses are arcs. You draw an arc by first drawing a circle and intersecting it with a line. Then you trim away the unwanted part of the circle. The other face of the lens is a mirror image of the first face. After you have drawn one lens, the remaining drawing is quite straightforward.

Figure 3-25
Optical Disk Pickup Schematic

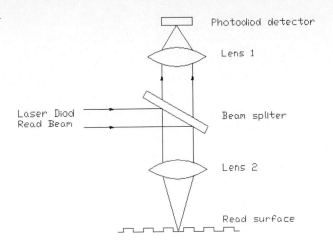

What If

What if the drawing is too long vertically? You can shorten the drawing by shortening the light rays between lens 1 and the reflecting mirror. Using a horizontal line as a cutting edge, trim the lines between the mirror and the lens. Finally, move the lens and the photodiode detector down. Use the top surface of the beam splitter as a boundary edge, and extend the vertical lines to intersect the mirror. You can use the same technique to shorten the lines between lens 2 and the beam splitter.

SUMMARY

In this chapter you've added several new editing tools to your repertoire. The Offset command is especially convenient if you need parallel or concentric copies of objects. You have learned how to extend and trim objects. You can copy, move, and mirror objects. Layers are a powerful tool you can use to organize a drawing. Linetypes and colors add a professional quality to the result. You can also change the properties of selected objects if you need to. Finally, the Redraw command permits you to refresh your screen, and the Zoom and Pan commands help you when you need to see details close up.

Key Words

base point	line scale
boundary edge	linetype
concentric	offset
current layer	optical disk pickup system
cutting edge	pan
extents	parallel
laser disk	symmetry
layer	zoom

Exercises

Reproduce the drawings shown in the following exercises. Do not try to add dimensions. Try to add simple arrowheads on the direction lines in the schematics.

Exercise 3-1
**Reflecting Telescope
Schematic**

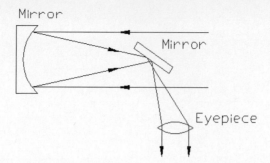

Exercise 3-2
Tool

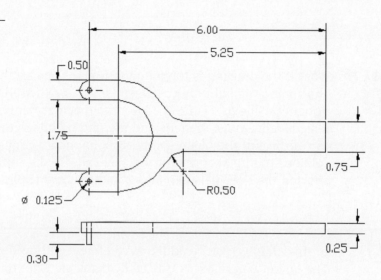

Exercise 3-3
Bracket

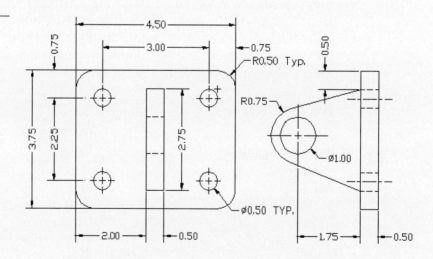

Exercise 3-4
Stair Detail

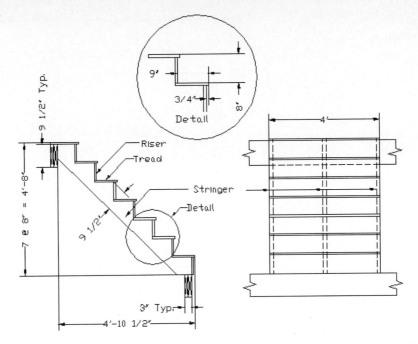

The thickness of the treads and risers is 3/4″. The thickness of the support beams is 2.5″. Offset and trim may be used to advantage in this problem.

Exercise 3-5
Printing Press Schematic Diagram

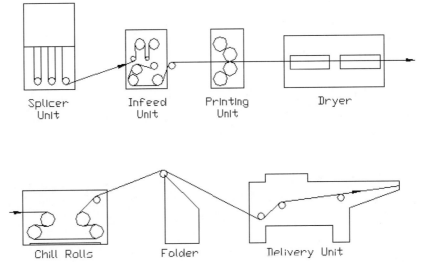

a. Adjust the limits to accommodate the overall length of the diagram. Dimensions of dryer: approximately 15′ by 7′.
b. Draw the elements approximately to scale, using these dimensions as a guide.
c. Use Copy and Mirror while drawing some of the elements. The lines representing the paper path are tangent to the rollers.

Exercise 3-6
Foundation Plan

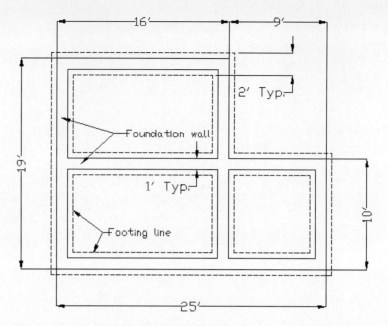

Select Engineering units. Set Upper Limits to 48′,36′. Set the Line Scale to 18.

a. Enter data with the foot (′) symbol.

b. Save this drawing because you will use it for an exercise in Chapter 5.

4 Using Additional Drawing and Editing Tools

Microprocessors Microprocessors are miniature computers that perform a wide range of functions. They are programmed to control anything from children's toys to automobile systems to remote sensing devices. The microprocessor is made from a combination of solid-state devices, the transistor being the oldest and most common. The microprocessor, fabricated as an integrated circuit, is encased in plastic for durability. Connecting pins are included in the assembly. The computer that you are using to run AutoCAD could not exist without microprocessors. CAD systems are used to design the integrated circuits employed in every modern electronic device, including computers. At the end of this chapter you will draw an electronic circuit designed to measure the operating characteristics of an element used in a microprocessor.

When using the 3 Points option, you simply select three points on the arc. Start the 3 Points option by clicking the button on the Draw toolbar. The first prompt is

```
Center/<Start point>:
```

Pick any point as the start point for the arc. The next prompt is

```
Center/End/<Second point>:
```

Again, pick any point as the second point on the arc. A rubber band forms after you pick the second point. You can see how the arc is being formed as you move the crosshairs around the screen. The prompt

```
End point:
```

appears. Pick the endpoint to complete the arc. Figure 4-2 illustrates a three-point arc.

Figure 4-2
3 Points Option of the Arc Command

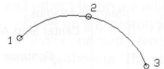

You can also draw an arc by specifying the start point, the center point, and the included angle. Two such arcs are shown in Figure 4-3. (The Arc command does not add the angular dimensions shown in the figure.) The included angle is the central angle of the arc (the angle between lines drawn from the center to the endpoints of the arc). You start this option by selecting the Start Center Angle button from the Arc pop-up menu.

The first prompt is

```
Center/<Start point>:
```

Pick any start point. AutoCAD remembers the order of the points (start and center) for this option, therefore the next prompt is

```
Center/End/<Second point>:
Center:
```

This seems to be a double prompt. AutoCAD remembers that you are using the Start Center Angle option and chooses the Center response automatically. Pick any point for the center of the arc. The next prompt is

```
Angle/Length of chord/<End point>:
Included angle:
```

Move the crosshairs to form an arc. You can pick a point with the mouse to establish an angle, but it is more common to enter a positive or negative angle from the keyboard.

Figure 4-3
**Start Center Angle
Option of the Arc
Command**

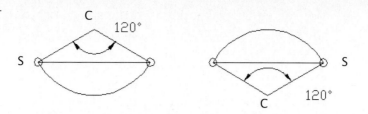

Figure 4-3
**Start Center Angle
Option of the Arc
Command**

Figure 4-3 also illustrates the effects of choosing a different start point (S) and center point (C). The angle is the same for each arc (+120 degrees). As you can see, the arc is drawn so that it goes from the start point to the endpoint in a counterclockwise direction.

You can also draw arcs using the Start End Radius option, which is illustrated in Figure 4-4. Select Start End Radius from the Arc pop-up menu and the prompt

        Center/<Start point>:

appears. Pick a start point for the arc. At the next prompt

        End point:

pick the endpoint. The next prompt is

        Angle/Direction/Radius/<Center point>:
        Radius:

You can enter the radius by moving the mouse until you are satisfied with the arc, but it is more common to type the value of the radius from the keyboard.

Figure 4-4
**Start End Radius
Option of the Arc
Command**

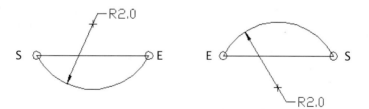

Drawing Rectangles and Other Polygons

To draw a rectangle, click the Rectangle button on the Draw toolbar. You are prompted to enter the diagonal corner points that define the rectangle (much like selecting the diagonal points that define the windows for zooming). The first prompt is

        First corner

Select the first corner point for the rectangle. At the next prompt

        Other corner

you can either pick a point on the screen or use relative coordinates (for example, @4,6) to construct the rectangle. AutoCAD then draws the rectangle the size you specified.

To draw an AutoCAD polygon, point to the Rectangle button on the Draw toolbar and hold down the left button on the mouse. Select the Polygon option on the resulting graphical pop-up menu. The first prompt is

```
Number of sides<default number>:
```

You can draw AutoCAD polygons with any number of sides between 3 and 1024. After you specify the number of sides, AutoCAD displays the prompt

```
Edge/<Center of polygon>:
```

This prompt allows you to specify the length and position of an edge, or to specify the center and radius of either a circumscribing or an inscribing circle. Figure 4-5 illustrates polygons drawn using these three options.

Figure 4-5
Polygon Options

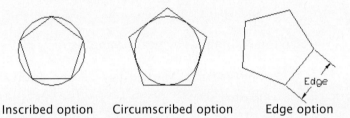

Inscribed option   Circumscribed option   Edge option

To choose the Center option, you pick a point on the screen. This point is the center of either an inscribing or circumscribing circle. AutoCAD displays the prompt

```
Inscribed in circle/Circumscribed about circle (I/C) <I>:
```

Type I to create an inscribed polygon or C to create a circumscribed polygon. Finally, AutoCAD presents the prompt

```
Radius of circle:
```

You supply a radius to complete the inscribed or circumscribed polygon.

If you select the Edge option by typing E and pressing (ENTER) at the

```
Edge/<Center of polygon>:
```

prompt, you are prompted in turn for the

```
First endpoint of edge:
```

and the

```
Second endpoint of edge:
```

By picking two points, you determine the size, location, and orientation of the polygon.

Drawing Ellipses

The ellipse is used in engineering drawings to show the view of a circle that you see if you look at the circle from an arbitrary direction. In Figure 4-6 the ellipse represents one view of a circle. The circle goes through the plate on the left. If you view the plate along line CB, you see the normal or orthographic view of the circle. Viewed from this direction the image of the circle is not distorted. If you look at the circle along line AB, however, the image of the circle is an ellipse.

Figure 4-6
Representing a Circle with an Ellipse

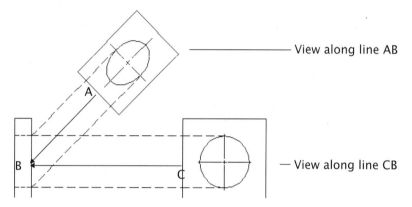

View along line AB

View along line CB

The ellipse is defined by two axes. The long or major axis is the diameter of the circle that the ellipse represents. The short or minor axis is the distorted length of the diameter of the circle. The ellipse is drawn by connecting the ends of two axes with a smooth curve.

You start the Ellipse command by pointing to the Ellipse button on the Draw toolbar and holding down the mouse's pick button. The resulting graphical pop-up menu has three options: Ellipse Center, Ellipse Axis End, and Ellipse Arc. You can select Ellipse Center to pick the center point and points on one end of each axis of the ellipse. Alternatively you can select Ellipse Axis End to pick points on both ends of one of the axes and then pick a point on one end of the other axis. We will not discuss the Ellipse Arc option in this text. If you are interested, you can experiment on your own to determine how elliptical arcs are created in AutoCAD. Figure 4-7 illustrates the two options used to create ellipses in AutoCAD.

Figure 4-7
Ellipse Options

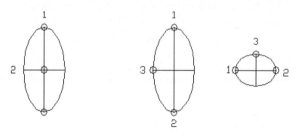

Ellipse Center option   Ellipse Axis End option

When you select the Ellipse Center button, AutoCAD displays the prompt

```
Arc/Center/<Axis endpoint 1>/_c
Center of ellipse:
```

Pick the center point. At the next prompt

```
Axis endpoint:
```

pick the end of one of the axes. Finally, at the prompt

```
<Other axis distance>/Rotation:
```

pick the end of the other axis.

When you select the Ellipse Axis End button, AutoCAD displays the prompt

```
Arc/Center/<Axis endpoint 1>:
```

Pick the end of one of the axes. At the prompt

```
Axis endpoint 2:
```

Pick the other end of the same axis. Finally, at the prompt

```
<Other axis distance>/Rotation:
```

pick either end of the other axis of the ellipse.

Adding Point Symbols to Your Drawing

Unlike the reference points that you pick when you are executing some commands, drawn points are real objects in a drawing. To issue the Point command, click the Point button on the Draw toolbar. AutoCAD displays the

```
Point:
```

prompt, and you pick a location for the drawn point. The point is invisible, however, unless you first set two values needed to make it visible.

There are two settings associated with points that you can change: point mode or symbol and point size. First choose **Display** from the **Option**s pull-down menu and then select **Point Style** from the next menu. The Point Style dialog box shown in Figure 4-8 appears. You can graphically select the symbol for your points by selecting the appropriate symbol from the top portion of the dialog box. You can change the size by entering a different number in the Point Size box. You can set the size in absolute units or as a percentage of the screen area. If you select absolute units, the size of the symbol changes when you change the screen display. If you make the size relative to the screen, the point appears unchanged as the screen display is changed. When you are satisfied with your selections, click OK.

Figure 4-8
Point Style Dialog Box

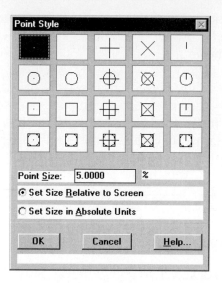

Try It   In this exercise you will begin to draw the top and front views of the
bracket shown in Figure 4-18. When you are finished with this exercise,
your drawing should look like the one shown below. (Note that your drawing will not contain the dimensions and notes shown on the figure.)

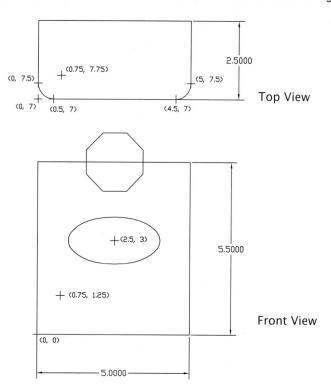

- ◆ Set the point style to the "cross" (+) and the point size to 2. Create the
  points labeled in the drawing. In the figure, the origin is shown as 0,0.
  Do not try to draw from the absolute origin, but start your drawing and
  then create the points relative to this origin.
- ◆ Create two rectangles for the top and front views. The rectangle for the
  front view should start at the point 0,0 and have the X and Y

dimensions shown. To pick a point, use the Object Snap option of Node. The rectangle for the top view should start at the point 0,7 and have the dimensions shown.

◆ Draw the two arcs in the top view by specifying the start and endpoints of each and a radius of 0.5. Trim away the corner part of the rectangle.

◆ Draw an eight-sided polygon (inscribed) that is centered at the midpoint of the upper line of the lower rectangle and has a radius of 1.0.

◆ Draw an ellipse by the Ellipse Center method. The center of the ellipse should be the center point of the front view. The first axis endpoint should be @1.5,0 and the second distance should be 0.75.

4-3   MANIPULATING OBJECTS

Often you will need to manipulate objects after you initially draw them. Using the Fillet and Chamfer commands you can modify corners of objects, which are usually drawn with sharp intersections. You can copy an object to a new location and change its size with the Scale command, which alters the size but not the shape of an object. If you need to change the shape of an object in a single direction, you use the Stretch command.

Using the Fillet Command

The Fillet command is designed to alter the intersection of lines or arcs. The command fillets, or rounds off, the corners with an arc tangent to the two objects. The original objects are trimmed back to the arc. Figure 4-9 illustrates the results of using the Fillet command on a pair of lines and on a line and an arc. The dashed lines represent the portion of the objects removed by the command. The fillet arc is labeled in the figure. As you can see, the Fillet command works even if the two objects do not actually intersect. The only requirement is that they would intersect if extended.

The Fillet command requires that you enter the radius of the arc before you select the objects. After setting the radius, you start the command again and select the objects.

Start the Fillet command by pointing to the Chamfer button on the Modify toolbar, holding down the left button on the mouse and then selecting the Fillet button on the resulting graphical pop-up menu. A mes-

Figure 4-9
Fillet Examples

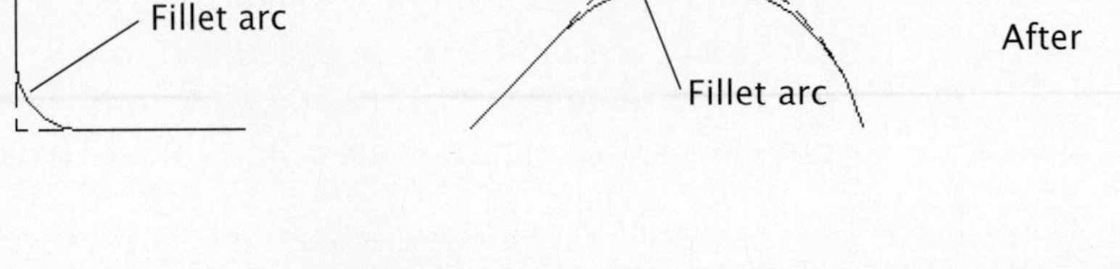

Before

Fillet arc

Fillet arc

After

sage will scroll, telling you what the current fillet radius is (if this is the first time you have activated the Fillet command it will be set to zero). At the prompt

```
Polyline/Radius/Trim/<Select first object>:
```

type R and press (ENTER) to signal that you will be entering or changing the radius. At the next prompt

```
Enter fillet radius <0.0000>:
```

enter the radius. The default value is 0.0000 unless you have set another value during the drawing session.

Click the Fillet button again to fillet two objects. At the prompt

```
Polyline/Radius/Trim/<Select first object>:
```

pick one of the lines or arcs you want to fillet. At the prompt

```
Select second object:
```

pick the other line or arc to fillet. AutoCAD will draw the fillet and end the command.

If the fillet radius is too large for the length of the lines, AutoCAD responds with the message "Radius is too large." If necessary, try again with a smaller radius.

The Fillet command works equally well on outside corners. In technical terms the fillets on outside corners are called *rounds*, and those on inside corners are called fillets. The arcs in the four inside corners of the lower-left object in Figure 4-10 are fillets. The arcs in the two outside corners are rounds.

Figure 4-10
Fillet and Round Examples

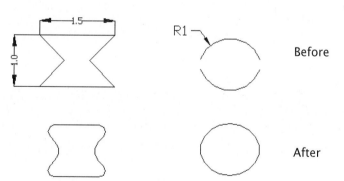

Using the Chamfer Command

The Chamfer command modifies the intersection of two lines (but not arcs) by *chamfering*, or cutting off the corner, or the intersection with a straight line. Chamfer requires two distances to determine how far back from the intersection to make the cut: The first distance is measured along the first line, and the second distance is measured along the second line.

The result of chamfering lines is illustrated in Figure 4-11. The drawings on the left use different chamfering distances. The lines on the right

Figure 4-11
Chamfer Examples

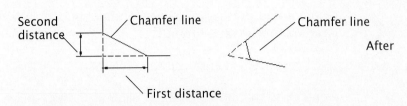

are chamfered with equal distances. Note that the lines do not need to intersect to be chamfered; AutoCAD finds the apparent intersection point and completes the chamfer. As with the Fillet command, to complete a chamfer process, you click the Chamfer button twice: once to set the chamfer distances and then again to chamfer the lines.

To start the Chamfer command, click the Chamfer button on the Modify toolbar. At the prompt

        Polyline/Distance/Angle/Trim/Method/<Select first line>:

type D and press (ENTER) to signal that you want to enter or change the distances.

At the prompt

        Enter first chamfer distance <0.0000>:

enter the first chamfer distance. The default value is 0.0000 if you are using the command for the first time in the drawing session. At the prompt

        Enter second chamfer distance <>:

enter the second distance. The default value for the second distance is the one you set for the first distance.

Once you have set the distances, click the Chamfer button again. At the prompt

        Polyline/Distance/Angle/Trim/Method/<Select first line>:

pick a line using the aperture. At the prompt

        Select second line:

pick another line. AutoCAD completes the chamfer and terminates the command. Since the chamfer operation trims the extra parts of the lines, the command does not work if a chamfer distance is too large. The command cannot eliminate an entire line.

enter the number of columns. At the prompt

```
Unit cell or distance between rows (---):
```

enter the vertical distance between corresponding points on the copies. At the prompt

```
Distance between columns (|||):
```

enter the horizontal distance between corresponding points on the copies. AutoCAD makes the copies and terminates the command.

The distances you enter can be positive or negative values. If you enter positive values, the copies are made to the right and above the original object. Negative distances cause the objects to be copied to the left and below the original. You can use any combination of signs to arrange the copies in the correct locations.

When you use the Unit cell option to set the distances, AutoCAD calculates the vertical and horizontal components of the line connecting the two points and uses them for the distances between rows and columns. For example, in Figure 4-13 the points A and B can be used as the two points. The dashed lines are shown to define the actual distances used by the Unit cell option. At the prompt

```
Unit cell or distance between rows (---):
```

pick a point and at the prompt

```
Other corner:
```

pick another point.

To create a polar array, choose the Polar Array button from the Copy Object graphical pop-up menu. At the prompt

```
Select objects:
```

pick the objects to be arrayed. At the prompt

```
Center point of array:
```

pick a point as the center of the imaginary circle. At the prompt

```
Number of items:
```

enter the number of final copies to be displayed. At the prompt

```
Angle to fill(+=ccw, -=cw) <360>:
```

enter an angle representing that portion of the imaginary circle to be filled. If you enter a negative angle, AutoCAD copies the objects in a clockwise direction about the center point. The magnitude of the angle determines the part of the circle that is to be filled. The resulting angular increment is equal to the total angle divided by the number of copies. At the prompt

```
Rotate objects as they are copied? <Y>:
```

type Y (for yes) to rotate the copies so that they have the same orientation to the center point as the original. Type N (for no) to have the copies maintain the same orientation with the coordinate axes as the original. Figure 4-15 illustrates the effect of the rotation response.

Figure 4-15
**Comparing Polar
Arrays**

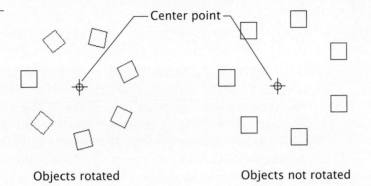

Objects rotated   Objects not rotated

Try It   In this exercise you will use the Rectangular Array and Polar Array commands to modify your drawing so that it looks like that shown below.

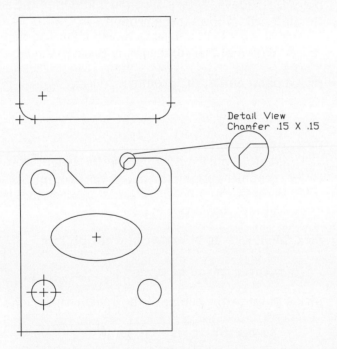

◆ Draw a circle centered at the lower-right point of the front view (it has coordinates of 0.75,1.25) which has a radius of 0.4.
◆ Create a rectangular array of this circle with two rows, two columns and a row and column spacing of 3.5.
◆ Draw a short horizontal line for one side of the center line for the circle. Make sure you leave a gap between the center point that you created in a previous Try It! exercise and the start of the line and that the line extends beyond the circle by a small amount (refer to the figure as necessary). Create a polar array of this small line about the center point with four items and an angle to fill of 360.

4-5   USING BLOCKS TO CREATE SYMBOL LIBRARIES

In Chapter 3 you drew the elements of a circuit diagram separately and then copied them to the proper location on the diagram and rotated them as necessary. You also placed the symbols on a separate layer that you could turn off when you were finished. This strategy is a primitive way of building a *symbol library*. The library is stored on the prototype drawing and is available only if you use that prototype. Furthermore, the symbols were made up of individual objects, and you must take care to select all of the components as you copy or move them.

Often it is easier to store all of the objects in a symbol as a group. In AutoCAD such symbols are called *blocks*. You can reuse a block in a drawing without using the Copy Object and Rotate commands. Windows, bolt heads, and symbols for trees and other plantings are examples of items frequently made into blocks.

Once a group of objects is made into a block and inserted into a drawing, it acts as a single object. Any editing command changes the entire block. The only way to separate the objects for individual editing is to explode the block, as discussed later in this section.

For example, Figure 4-16 shows the floor plan of an office suite that includes a reception area, an executive office, a conference room, and a variety of furniture, including tables, chairs, desks, file cabinets, and book cases. Each item was created separately as a block. Each block was then inserted into the floor plan. The location, size, and orientation of the items were set while the block was being inserted.

Figure 4-16
Interior Design of an Office Suite

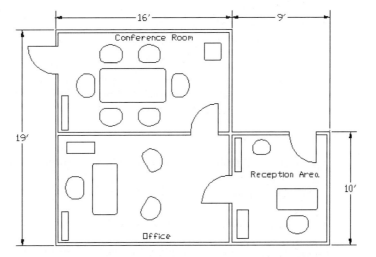

Creating Blocks

You create a block by pointing to the Insert Block button on the Draw toolbar, holding down the mouse's left button, and selecting the Block button on the resulting graphical pop-up menu. By default blocks are stored in the current drawing file, but you can create Wblocks which are stored in separate external files. (You will learn how to create Wblocks later in this section.) Later you can use the Insert Block command to retrieve the blocks and place them in a drawing.

When you select the Block command, you are asked to assign a name to the block, select the objects to be included, and pick a base point. The base point for a block is similar to the base point designated in the Copy Object command: It is the point that locates the position of the block when it is copied into the drawing.

To issue the Block command, choose the Block button from the Insert Block graphical pop-up menu. At the prompt

```
Block name (or ?):
```

enter the name of the new block, or type ? to see a list of existing blocks. At the prompt

```
Insertion base point:
```

pick a point to serve as the base point when the block is inserted later. This point is also the point about which rotations take place during the insert step. Finally, at the prompt

```
Select objects:
```

select the objects to be included in the block.

When you have completed the selection, the information is added to the drawing file, and the objects disappear from the screen. If you need some or all of the objects for further work in the drawing, you can recover them by typing OOPS at the command line.

The Block command places the block in the drawing file, where it is accessible only from the drawing in which it was created. If you want to be able to use the block in other drawings, you must use the Wblock command. You initiate the Wblock command by typing WBLOCK at the command line. The Create New Drawing File dialog box appears. This dialog box is essentially the same as the Select File dialog box. To name the Wblock, type the name in the Filename text box. Select the directory or drive for the Wblock file by scrolling up or down the Directories list box until the name comes into view and clicking the desired directory. Click OK to leave the dialog box. At the next prompt

```
Block name:
```

press (ENTER) to use the file name you typed in the File Name box of the dialog box. The block is written to the file with the .DWG extension. Follow the procedure as outlined previously for the specification of the block geometry to be written to the Wblock.

Inserting Blocks into a Drawing

The Insert Block button allows you to copy a block into a drawing, scale it in both the horizontal and vertical directions, and rotate it, all in one step.

When you select the Insert Block button from the Draw toolbar, AutoCAD displays the Insert dialog box shown in Figure 4-17. To insert a block that is local to the current drawing, click the Block button. Another dialog box appears listing all of the available blocks within the drawing.

Select the name of the block you want and click OK to insert that block name in the text box in the Insert dialog box. To insert a Wblock, click the File button, and in the next dialog box, select the path (the drive name and directories) with the file name where the drawing resides. The name of the block appears in the space to the right of the File button in the Insert dialog box.

Next, if you know them from information in the drawing, you can specify the coordinates of the insertion point, the scale factors, and the angle. You can change data in any parameter box by clicking the box and typing the new data. When you finish entering all the parameters you want, click OK and the command terminates. When you click the Specify Parameters on Screen box, you can set the parameters as you are inserting the block into the drawing.

If you do not know the exact coordinates of the insertion point in advance, you can insert the block by specifying the parameters on the screen and then moving the block as needed. Click OK, and a sequence of prompts appears. At the first prompt

```
Insertion point:
```

pick a point where the base point is to be inserted. Moving the crosshairs moves the image of the block on the screen. AutoCAD displays the prompt

```
X scale factor <1>/Corner/XYZ:
```

The XYZ option allows you to change all three scales of three-dimensional blocks. The Corner option is beyond the scope of this text. For two-dimensional blocks, you can either press (ENTER) to accept the default X scale factor of 1 or enter a different X scale factor. At the prompt

```
Y scale factor (default = X):
```

you can either press (ENTER) to accept the default value or enter a different Y scale factor. At the last prompt

```
Rotation angle <0>:
```

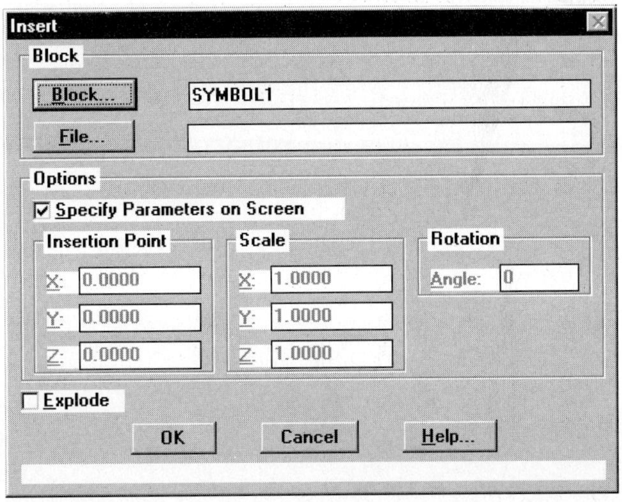

Figure 4-17
Insert Dialog Box

you can either press (ENTER) to accept the default value or enter a different value. A negative angle rotates the image counterclockwise about the insertion point.

Using the Explode Command to Edit Blocks

After you have made a group of objects into a block and inserted it into a drawing, you cannot edit individual objects in the group. For example, you cannot erase one line of a group of lines in a block. If you need to do so, you must first use the Explode command to explode, or separate, the objects. Then you can edit the individual objects easily. You can use the Explode command on other objects that act as blocks, such as polygons, polylines, and the components of dimensions, (as discussed in the Chapter 5).

To issue the Explode command, click the Explode button on the Modify toolbar. At the prompt

```
Select objects:
```

select the objects to be exploded using any selection technique. As you select the objects, notice that their appearance changes. When you have completed the selection, the objects are ready for editing on an individual basis.

Try It In this exercise you will complete your drawing so that it looks like the one shown in Figure 4-18.

- ◆ Create two concentric circles in the top view centered at the point you created with radii of 0.4 and 0.45. Change the linetype of the outer circle to Hidden2 (make sure the linetype is loaded first).
- ◆ Convert these two circles to a block with an insertion point at their center (do not include the point as part of the block). Insert the block in the original location as well as in the location on the opposite side of the top view (using a location of @3.5,0 for the second block is probably easiest). Use a scale factor of 1 in both directions and a rotation of zero for both locations.
- ◆ Erase all of the construction points on the drawing except for the one defining the center lines for the circle in the lower left corner of the front view.
- ◆ Create a Wblock out of the circle center lines and point. Use the file name CIRCEN and specify the point as the insertion point for the block. You will now have this symbol available to you for any other drawing you create using AutoCAD.
- ◆ Insert this symbol at each of the six small circles in the drawing (four in the front view and two in the top view).
- ◆ Explode the top rectangle to break it into smaller pieces. Offset the top and bottom lines of the two rectangles each by 0.5 to the inside of the drawing.

Figure 4-18
Top and Front Views of Bracket

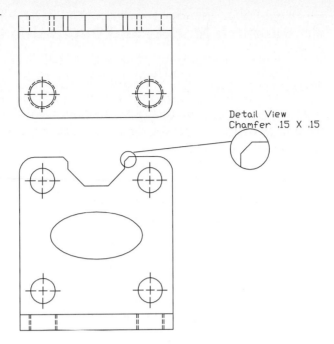

◆ Add hidden and visible lines as needed to complete the drawing. It is probably easiest to offset the side lines and trim them away accordingly. The offset distances in the front view are 0.3, 0.35, 1.15, and 1.2 from each side. The offset distances in the top are 0.35, 1.0, 1.15, 1.45, 1.60, and 2.15 from each side.

◆ Change the properties of the appropriate offset lines you just created so that they have a Hidden2 linetype and they are located on the Hide drawing layer.

Application 3   DIGITAL ELECTRONICS CIRCUIT

Electrical and Electronics Engineering

Digital electronic circuits are designed to perform a wide variety of tasks in the computer and communications industries. Before any electronic instrument goes into production, performance tests are conducted to certify that the instrument meets or exceeds its advertised specifications. The same sort of testing begins at the most basic level, the individual elements in the instrument. This application is the design of a circuit to test the transfer characteristic of a solid-state device, known as the 7400 TTL NAND gate.

You can use the five-step problem-solving process to draw the circuit diagram.

1. Identify the Object and Its Function

The circuit is designed so that one voltage on the input side of the NAND gate can be varied while the other voltage on the input side remains constant. The circuit provides a way of measuring the voltage on the output side of the gate. The data, the variable input voltages and the corresponding output voltages will be read, recorded, and plotted.

2. Research Models and Determine Dimensions

There may be several ways of arranging the circuit so that it satisfies the needs of the experiment. You need to do a little research in a standard electronics textbook to become familiar with the NAND gate. In addition, you need to choose the device to control the voltages on the input side of the gate as well as measuring the output voltage. You will probably be able to use a standard variable resistance in combination with a fixed resistance voltage source to vary the input resistance. You can use a multimeter to measure the fixed input voltage as well as the variable output resistance.

 ## 3. Make a Hand-drawn Sketch

Use Figure 4-19 as the basis for your rough sketch. The circuit diagram includes a resistor, a ground symbol, and a repeated node symbol. It is important to plan the size of the symbols and the lengths of the connecting elements so that the finished drawing looks professional. You can add the text after drawing the circuit diagram. Make sure that the height and style of the text are in proportion to the rest of the drawing.

Figure 4-19
**Circuit Diagram for
Testing a NAND Gate**

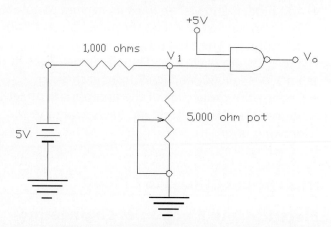

 ## 4. Make Appropriate Screen Adjustments

Set up a prototype drawing called CIRCUITS. Make a layer for the text and name it Text. Make another layer, called Elem, on which to draw the basic elements and convert them to blocks before you copy them to the proper locations in the circuit diagram. You will turn off this layer when you have completed the diagram. For the different layers, set colors that are comfortable for you to look at. Save the prototype drawing after you create the blocks but before you draw any part of the diagram. Start a new drawing, called CIRC1, using the CIRCUITS prototype.

 ## 5. Draw, Print or Plot, and Save the File

Draw the actual circuit on Layer 0, and add the text to the Text layer. When you have completed the drawing, compare it to Figure 4-19 and save and print or plot the file.

What If

What if you discovered that you drew the circuit diagram on the Elem layer? How would you correct the error?

What if the elements in the diagram were too close together to accommodate the text clearly? How would you move the elements apart without redrawing them or using the Move command?

SUMMARY

In this chapter you learned how to set up prototype drawings that include layers, units, limits, colors, and other settings. You have added to your collection of drawing and editing tools so you can now draw arcs, ellipses, polygons, and rectangles. You can use new editing commands—Fillet, Chamfer, Scale, and Stretch—to draw increasingly complex objects. You can also copy objects in either rectangular or polar arrays. Finally you can use blocks to create complicated symbols you use repeatedly on your drawings.

Key Words

arc	polar array
block	polygon
border	prototype drawing
chamfer	rectangle
circumscribe	rectangular array
ellipse	reference length
explode	round
fillet	scale factor
included angle	stretch
inscribe	symbol library
major axis	title block
minor axis	Wblock

Exercises

Reproduce the following drawings using the given dimensions when they are provided. Do not add dimensions, but reproduce the text whenever possible. Use a prototype drawing when appropriate.

Exercise 4-1
Custom Switch Plate

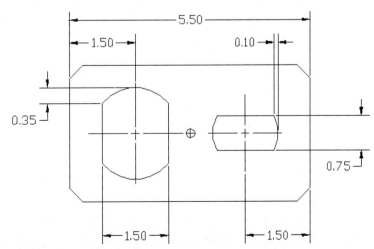

Center Hole diameter = 0.2
Chamfer Distance = 0.25

Exercise 4-2A
Fixture

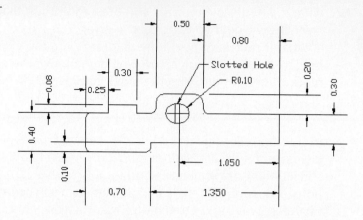

Figure 4-2B
Slotted Hole Detail

Exercise 4-3
Wrench

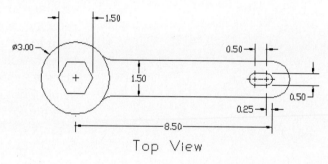

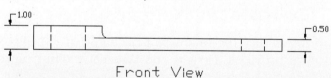

a. Draw the two views of the wrench as shown in Exercise 4-3.
b. Save the drawing.
c. Increase the length of the handle by 1/2 inch without changing any of
   the other dimensions.

Exercise 4-4
Circuit Diagram

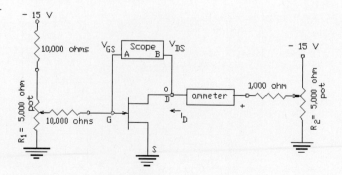

Use the CIRCUIT prototype, and add the new element symbols as blocks to
the Elem layer as shown in Exercise 4-4.

Exercise 4-5
**Schematic for
Producing Solid CO2**

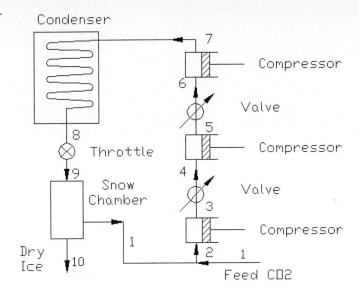

a. Draw the compressor and valves as blocks.
b. Draw a line with arrows to use as a block on the drawing.

Exercise 4-6
Gasket

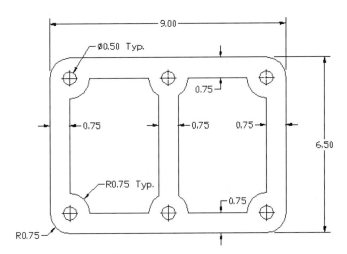

a. Draw the gasket as shown in Exercise 4-6.
b. Save the drawing.
c. Change the length from 9 to 11.5 and the height from 6.5 to 8. The new gasket is symmetrical about the center holes.

Exercise 4-7
**Standard Bolt with
Square Head and Nut**

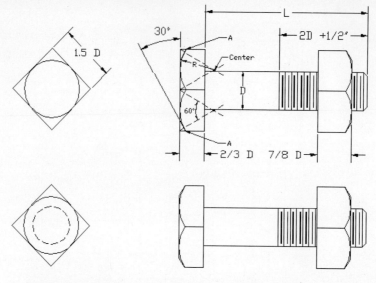

a. Draw the square as a polygon and the outline of the bolt head thickness, using the dimensions of a 1-inch–diameter bolt.
b. Draw the 60-degree dashed lines from the corners of bolt head.
c. Draw circles with centers at the intersections of the dashed lines and tangent to the top of the head. Trim the circles as shown.
d. Draw 30-degree lines from point A, and draw lines to finish the outline of the head.
e. Mirror the head to form part of the nut. Add the rest of the nut, the bolt shaft, and the thread symbols.
f. Copy the result to the lower position before erasing the dashed construction lines.
g. Erase the construction lines on the lower image.

Exercise 4-8
Circuit Diagram

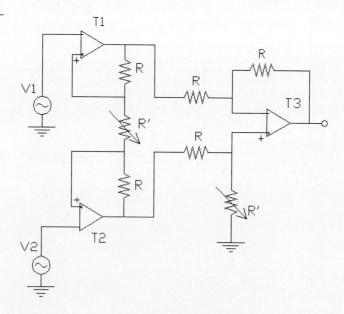

Create the drawing of the circuit diagram using symbols and blocks as necessary.

5 Adding Annotation to Your Drawing

Composite Materials Composites combine different materials in a matrix to take advantage of the strengths of the separate materials. An early example of a composite material is reinforced brick made from straw and mud. The tensile strength of the straw kept the brick from cracking. Modern reinforced concrete is a direct descendent of reinforced bricks. Steel reinforcing bars replaced the straw, and concrete replaced the mud. Even more interesting are composites that use carbon and glass fibers in an epoxy matrix. These composites are strong and lightweight. The combination of strength, light weight, and heat resistance is especially suited to applications in aircraft and space vehicles. At the end of this chapter, you will draw a modern bicycle wheel made of carbon, Kevlar, and glass fibers molded over a foam core.

INTRODUCTION

This chapter introduces you to the addition of drawing annotation. Drawing annotation consists of information other than the lines, arcs, circles, or other geometric objects that make up a drawing. The three major types of drawing annotation are crosshatching, text, and dimensions. You have already learned the basics of adding text to your drawing, but in this chapter you will explore some of the more specialized methods for adding and editing text. You will also discover how to add crosshatching to clarify the interior details of parts. You learn how to use the Measure and Divide commands to draw points at evenly spaced distances along lines, circles, and arcs. Finally, you learn how to add dimensions and labels to the objects in your drawings.

5-1 ADDING TEXT TO DRAWINGS

Text is an essential part of all engineering drawings. For example, you use text to describe the materials to be used and to add *title blocks* which indicate who prepared the drawing.

Adding text to a drawing involves two steps. First you use one of the Text commands to insert the text, placing it in the correct location on the drawing, aligning it, and adjusting its size. Second you use the Style commands to design the text style, selecting the appearance of the characters, choosing the height-to-width ratio, and picking the slope and orientation of the characters.

AutoCAD provides three options you can use to add text to your drawing: Text (also called MText), DText, and Single-Line Text. Text consists of a block of text which is treated as a single object within AutoCAD. You can type the text as a single paragraph or as multiple paragraphs. Text is similar to using a wordprocessor. Within a paragraph, the text wraps from one line to the next as you type. You can resize the borders as needed to change the look of the text on your drawing. DText (dynamic text) consists of several single lines of text aligned along one side. When you use DText, AutoCAD displays the text on the screen as you are typing so you can judge the length of the lines. You can also continue the text on multiple lines by pressing (ENTER) at the end of each line. With DText each individual line of text is treated as a separate object by AutoCAD, unlike MText where all lines of a block of text are treated as a single object. Single lines of text are added to drawings as single objects.

All of the text commands are found in the Text graphical pop-up menu on the Draw toolbar. When you click the Text button on the Draw toolbar, the following prompt appears:

```
Attach/Rotation/Style/Height/Direction/<Insertion Point>:
```

You then select a point on the drawing to define a corner of the border for the block of text. At the next prompt

```
Attach/Rotation/Style/Height/Direction/Width/2Points/
<Other Corner>:
```

you can select the other corner point of the text border (much like selecting the two corner points of a window or a rectangle). The Edit MText dialog box appears as shown in Figure 5-1.

Figure 5-1
Edit MText Dialog Box

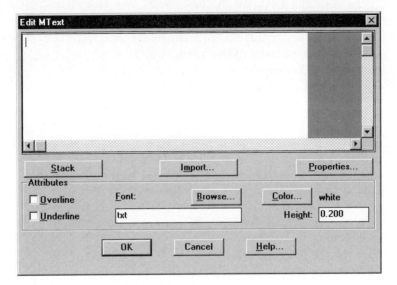

You enter text in the large white box in the upper half of the dialog box. The size of the box will vary depending on how big you made your selection window on your drawing. If you click the Import button, you can bring an externally created text file into your document. You use the options in the Attributes area of the Edit MText dialog box to change the color, height, font or other attributes of the text. When you click the Properties button on the dialog box, the MText Properties dialog box shown in Figure 5-2 appears.

Figure 5-2
**MText Properties
Dialog Box**

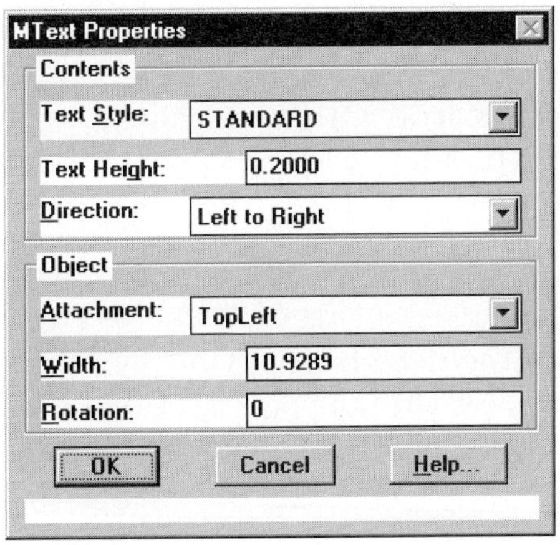

You can change the text style or height in the MText Properties dialog box. You can also choose to align text from left to right or from top to bottom. You control the properties of the object (text block) from this dialog box. Note that you can change the width of the text box as well as its rotation angle.

When you are finished entering your block of text within the Edit MText dialog box, click OK and your text will be placed on your drawing at the location you specified. You can then move or copy the paragraph of text around on your drawing much as you modify geometric objects.

Instead of adding a block of text to your drawing, you can add multiple lines that are aligned along one side. This is called DText in AutoCAD. When you point to the Text button on the Draw tool bar, hold down the mouse's left button and select the DText button from the resulting graphical pop-up menu, the main DText prompt appears:

```
Justify/Style/<Start point>:
```

If you choose the default (Start point) option, the lines of text will be left justified. Choose the Style option to change from one style to another. You can initiate the Justify option by typing J at this prompt and pressing (ENTER); another prompt appears offering you 14 more options for justifying text.

The Start point and Justify options of the DText command are discussed in detail in this section.

Using the Start Point Option   The Start point option results in left-justified text, as illustrated in Figure 5-3. The plus sign (+) in this and subsequent figures indicates the justification points of the lines of text. It does not appear when you enter text but is shown to identify where the text lines up with the points you select when you start a line of text.

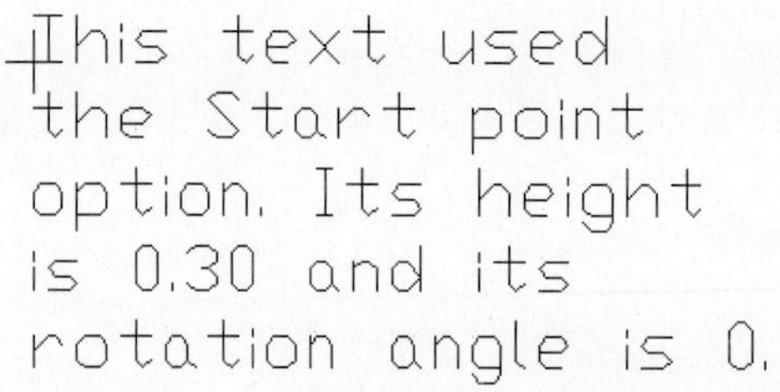

Figure 5-3
DText Using the Start Point Option

This text used
the Start point
option. Its height
is 0.30 and its
rotation angle is 0.

To initiate the Start point option, you select a start point for the text at the main DText prompt, using any selection technique. The start point is indicated by the + in Figure 5-3. The following prompt appears:

```
Height <0.2000>:
```

The number is the default height of the characters and is equal to the value that was used with the last DText command. Type a new value and press (ENTER), or press (ENTER) to accept the default value. The next prompt is

```
Rotation Angle <0>:
```

The rotation angle is the angle the text line makes with the horizontal. Enter a new value, or press (ENTER) to accept the default value of zero. After you set the angle, a square the size of the characters appears at the start point. At the final prompt

```
Text:
```

type the text. You can enter multiple lines of text by pressing (ENTER) at the end of each line. Press (ENTER) twice to end the DText command.

Alternatively, you can choose Justify at the main DText prompt and then choose from among the many justification options presented to you on the next menu. The Align, Fit, Center, Middle, and Right options of the Justify command are discussed in this section. The other options are beyond the scope of this text.

You can use the Align option to align text between two points in the drawing. These points set the slope of the text line, and the text is forced to fit between the points. The Align option does not prompt you for a height. Instead the height is adjusted depending on the number of characters in the line of text. Figure 5-4 illustrates the Align option, showing the effects of choosing different distances between the two aligning points.

Figure 5-4
**Align Option of the
Justify Command**

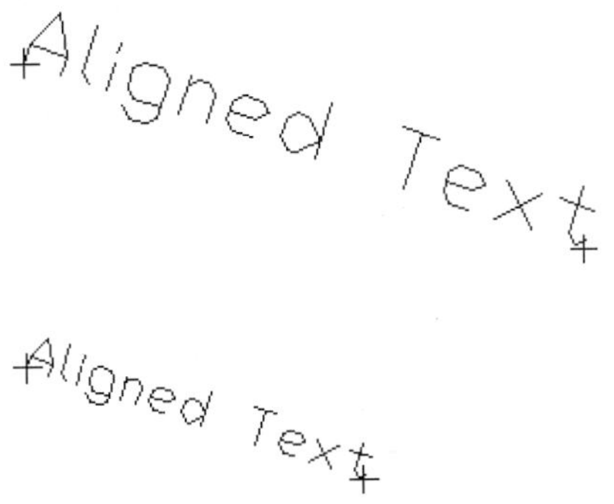

To initiate the Align option, type J and press (ENTER) at the

```
Justify/Style/<Start point>:
```

prompt. At the next prompt,

```
Align/Fit/Center/Middle/Right/TL/TC/TR/ML/MC/MR/BL/BC/BR:
```

type **A** and press (ENTER). The next prompt is

```
First text line point:
```

Pick a point on the screen, and the prompt

```
Second text line point:
```

appears. Pick a second point to fix the alignment. AutoCAD displays a small square showing the alignment of the characters. At the prompt

```
Text:
```

you can type the text. After you enter the text, the size of the characters is adjusted to fill the distance between the two points. At the "Text:" prompt, if you enter some text, press (ENTER), and then continue typing text on a second line, the characters on the two lines will have different sizes.

The Fit option is illustrated in Figure 5-5. It is similar to Align with one major difference: The height of the characters is fixed. The width of the characters is adjusted to fit the line of text between the two text points.

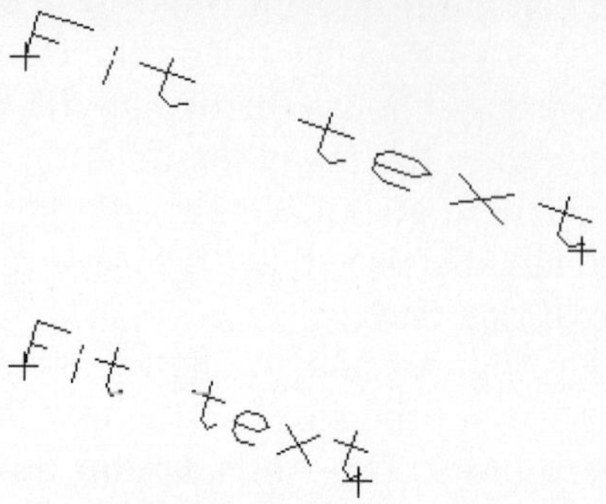

Figure 5-5
**Fit Option of the
Justify Command**

Fit text

Fit text

To initiate the Fit option, type J and press (ENTER) at the main DText prompt. At the prompt

    Align/Fit/Center/Middle/Right/TL/TC/TR/ML/MC/MR/BL/BC/BR:

type F and press (ENTER). The next prompt is

    First text line point:

Pick a point on the screen, and the prompt

    Second text line point:

appears. Pick a second point to fix the alignment. At the prompt

    Height <0.2000>:

enter a new height or accept the default value, and a small square appears. At the prompt

    Text:

type the text, pressing (ENTER) twice when you're done. AutoCAD adjusts the characters to fill the distance between the two points.

The Center and Middle options are very similar. Each prompts you for a point and centers the text horizontally about that point (if the rotation angle is 0). The Center option centers the text above an imaginary line through the point. The Middle option centers the characters vertically about the point. These options are illustrated in Figure 5-6.

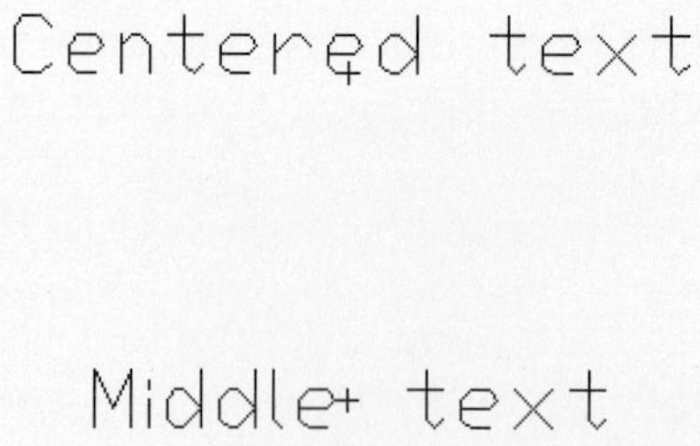

Figure 5-6
**Middle and Center
Options of the Justify
Command**

Centered text

Middle text

To initiate the Center option, type J and press (ENTER) at the

```
Justify/Style/<Start point>:
```

prompt. At the prompt

```
Align/Fit/Center/Middle/Right/TL/TC/TR/ML/MC/MR/BL/BC/BR:
```

type C and press (ENTER). The next prompt is

```
Center point:
```

Pick a center point with the mouse or enter the coordinates from the keyboard. At the prompt

```
Height <0.2000>:
```

enter the height. At the prompt

```
Rotation angle <0>:
```

enter the rotation angle. A small square appears to show the size of the characters, and the prompt

```
Text:
```

appears. Enter the text as before. The text temporarily appears to the right of the center point. After you press (ENTER) twice, the text shifts to the left and centers itself around the center point.

To initiate the Middle option, type J and press (ENTER) at the

```
Justify/Style/<Start point>:
```

prompt. At the prompt

```
Align/Fit/Center/Middle/Right/TL/TC/TR/ML/MC/MR/BL/BC/BR:
```

type M and press (ENTER). The next prompt is

```
Middle point:
```

Pick a point to serve as the middle point for your text. Then enter a height and a rotation angle, and enter your text, as you did with the Center option, pressing (ENTER) twice when you're done. The plus (+) marks in Figure 5-6 show how the text is positioned vertically about the center and middle points.

The Right option illustrated in Figure 5-7 allows you to right justify lines of text. You select a point that establishes the right edge of the text. As you type the text, it temporarily appears to the right of the selected point. When you press (ENTER) twice, the text shifts to the left and becomes right justified.

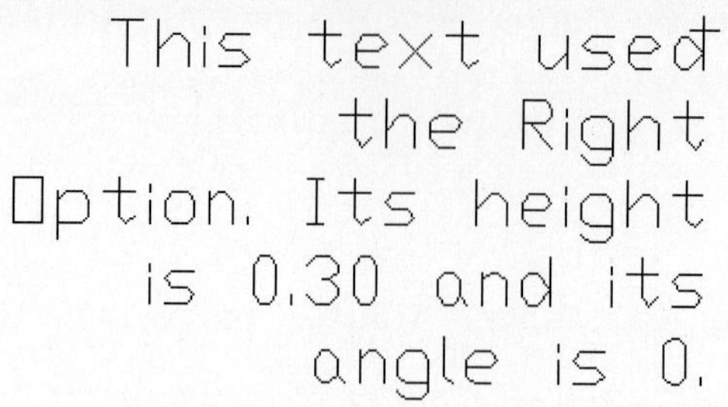

Figure 5-7
**Right Option of the
Justify Command**

This text used
the Right
Option. Its height
is 0.30 and its
angle is 0.

To initiate the Right option, type J and press (ENTER) at the

    Justify/Style/<Start point>:

prompt. At the prompt

    Align/Fit/Center/Middle/Right/TL/TC/TR/ML/MC/MR/BL/BC/BR:

type R and press (ENTER). At the prompt

    Endpoint:

pick a point to serve as the right end of the lines of text. The prompt

    Height <0.2000>:

appears. After you enter the height, AutoCAD displays the prompt

    Rotation angle <0>:

Enter the rotation angle and the prompt

    Text:

appears. Enter the text, pressing (ENTER) twice to complete the command.

Try It

For the Try It! exercises in this chapter you will be creating a drawing of a typical approach for a section of highway. The drawing you will be creating is shown in Figure 5-25.
- Start a new drawing, and set the Units to Engineering with a precision of 0'-0" and angles reported in Deg/Min/Sec with a direction of Clockwise. Set the upper right limits of the drawing to 600',300' (make sure to include the ' so the numbers will be interpreted as feet and not inches). Change your view to zoom the drawing limits.
- Enter the following block of text for the drawing as MText:
THE PROPOSED PAVEMENT SHALL BE 9-INCH THICK REINFORCED CON-CRETE PAVEMENT WITH 7-INCH INTEGRAL STRAIGHT CURB HAVING A 5-INCH PARABOLIC CROWN.
THE COST OF REMOVING CONCRETE PAVEMENT WILL BE PAID FOR AS SPECIFIED IN THE PROPOSAL.THE COST OF REMOVAL OF BITUMINOUS PAVEMENT AND DRIVES SHALL BE INCIDENTAL TO THE PROJECT.
- Change the size of the text and the text box border so that this text appears correctly on the drawing (a text height of around 50 and a

width of text box of around 2000 will work well). Move the block of text so that it is located in the upper-right portion of the drawing.
◆ Create the following lines of text as left-justified DText on your drawing somewhere near the MText you just created. Specify a text height equal to the height you specified in the previous block of text.
WATER MAIN CONSTRUCTION
ALL WATER MAIN PIPE SHALL BE 12" IN DIAMETER.
WATER MAIN BEDDING SHALL BE CLASS II SAND.
WATER MAIN TRENCH BACKFILL SHALL BE TRENCH "A" (SAND).
WHENEVER THE CONTRACTOR NEEDS TO SHUT OFF A WATER MAIN, THE CONTRACTOR SHALL NOTIFY THE CITY.
◆ Change the height of the first line of DText to twice that of the remaining text.
◆ Add your name and class section number as right-justified text in the upper-left corner of the drawing screen.

Creating New Text Styles

So far you have been using AutoCAD's Standard text style. You can, however, create as many new styles as you need for a given drawing. To define a new text style, you must name the style; choose a font; set the height, the width factor, and an obliquing angle; and, finally, decide whether you want the characters to be backward, upside-down, or arranged in a vertical line. An advantage of creating new styles is that, if you redefine any part of a previously defined style, all of the text entered in that style is changed automatically.

To begin creating a new text style, choose **Text Style** from the **Data** pull-down menu. AutoCAD displays the prompt

        Text style name (or ?)<STANDARD>:

The name in angle brackets is the current style. It will be the Standard style, unless you have been using another style. Enter a name for the new style, and the Select Font File dialog box shown in Figure 5-8 appears. To see the names of the available fonts, scroll through the File Name list box. When you find the font that fits your needs, click on its name and then click OK. The message "New Style" appears in the command area, and the dialog box disappears.

Figure 5-8
**Select Font File
Dialog Box**

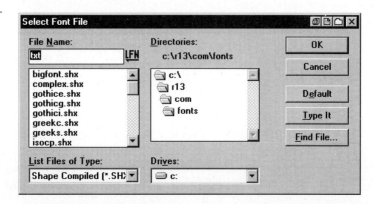

The next prompt is

```
Height <0.0000>:
```

Enter a height or accept the default value. If you enter 0, you are prompted for the height when you enter text. If you enter any other value, the height is fixed. It is better practice to enter 0 so you can adjust the height when you enter text.

At the next prompt

```
Width factor <1.000>:
```

enter a value or accept the default value. This factor controls the ratio of the width to the height of the letters. The default value is 1, but you can use other values for special effects. For most engineering applications a width factor of 1 is standard. The next prompt is

```
Obliquing angle <0>:
```

You can either enter an angle or press (ENTER) to accept the default value. A positive value slants the letters to the right, and a negative value slants the letters to the left. For engineering drawings it is standard to accept the default value of zero, which results in upright letters.

At the prompt

```
Backwards? <N>:
```

enter Y if you want the text to read backward. Otherwise, accept the default value of N. The next prompt is

```
Upside-down? <N>:
```

Enter Y if you want the text to appear upside-down. Otherwise, accept the default value of N. At the next prompt

```
Vertical? <N>:
```

enter Y if you want the text to read vertically. Otherwise, accept the default value of N. If you need to enter a label along the edge of a drawing, vertical text is useful.

When you have responded to these prompts, the message

```
style is now the current text style
```

appears, where *style* is the name you used at the first prompt.

Figure 5-9 illustrates a variety of styles. The New style has no unusual characteristics. New1 is a vertical style, and New2 is backward.

Changing Text Styles After you have created one or more text styles, you can use these styles instead of the Standard style that AutoCAD provides. To change to a new style when entering MText, click the Properties button on the Edit MText dialog box and then choose the style you want

Figure 5-9
Comparing New Text Styles

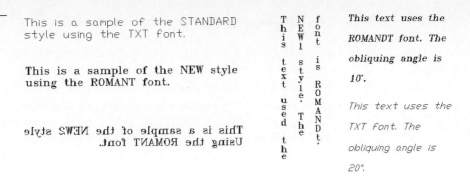

from the Text Style list box (refer back to Figures 5-1 and 5-2). To change to a new style when entering DText, at the prompt

        Justify/Style/<Start point>:

type S and press ⒺⓃⓉⒺⓇ. The prompt

        Style name (or?)<STANDARD>:

appears. Type the name of the new style and press ⒺⓃⓉⒺⓇ. The prompt

        Justify/Style/<Start point>:

reappears. Continue to enter text using the new style. If you do not remember the style names that you created, type ? and press ⒺⓃⓉⒺⓇ to display the list of style names. The default style name will be the last style that you used.

Creating Special Characters with Control Codes

A number of special characters are common in engineering drawings, including the degree symbol (°), the tolerance symbol (±), the percent symbol (%), and the diameter (ø) symbol. To create these symbols and underscore or overscore text, you type the special control codes shown in Table 5-1 as a part of the text. When you are finished, AutoCAD will convert the control codes you entered into the symbols shown in the table.

Table 5-1   Special Control Codes

Symbol	Control Code Sample Entry	Effect
¯ (overscore)	%%OOverscore%%O	Overscore
_ (underscore)	%%UUnderscore%%U	Underscore
° (degree)	230%%D	230°
± (tolerance)	4.5%%P0.01	4.5±0.01
ø (diameter)	%%C 2.5	ø 2.5
% (percent)	50 %%%	50 %

Other codes exist for you to use in AutoCAD. For a complete list of the available codes, please check the AutoCAD documentation.

Modifying Text

You can modify text that you have entered on your drawing by moving, copying, or rotating it using the appropriate button on the Modify toolbar. You can also change the attributes of the text such as its height, style, layer, rotation, and so on by choosing **Properties** from the **Edit** pull-down menu. If you select a single block of text as the object to modify, the Modify Text dialog box shown in Figure 5-10 appears (this is similar to the Modify Line dialog box shown in Figure 3-18). You can modify the actual text by clicking in the Text box and retyping the text as you want it to appear. You can apply a new style to the text or change any of its other attributes by making appropriate selections in the lower portion of the dialog box. When you are finished making changes, click OK to change the attributes of the text on your drawing.

Figure 5-10
Modify Text Dialog Box

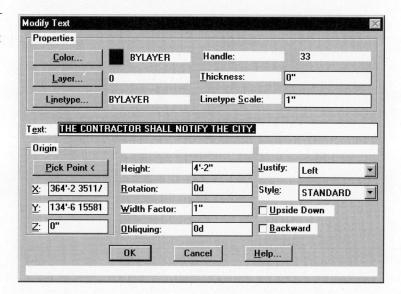

Try It ◆ Create a new text style with the Romant font and an obliquing angle of 10°. Using a text height of 75, add a drawing title consisting of "Typical Approach Treatment Detail 1" at the bottom of the drawing.
◆ Modify the line of DText with the diameter of water main pipe specified so that it reads "ALL WATER PIPES SHALL BE Ø12."

5-2   USING HATCH PATTERNS

The Hatch command enables you to use a hatch pattern—one of any number of line or fill patterns—to highlight an area of your drawing. The most common use of hatch patterns in engineering drawings is to clarify the interior geometric details of a part in a sectional view. The hatch pattern can also indicate the material used in manufacturing the part.

Figure 5-11 shows a plate drawn in front, right side, and sectional views. As you can see, the hatched sectional view clarifies the interior detail more easily than hidden lines would. The hidden lines in the right

Figure 5-11
**Using a Hatch Pattern
in a Sectional Drawing**

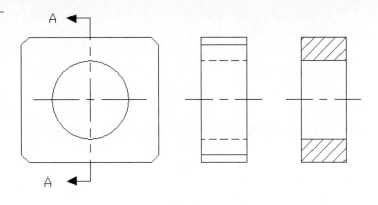

Front view   Right side view   Sectional view

side view of the plate show that the hole penetrates entirely through the plate. At times, however, the interior details of the part are not so obvious. To expose the interior details, the part is cut by an imaginary plane and the material in front of that plane is removed to produce a sectional view. In sectional views the areas of the object that were intersected by the cutting plane are cross hatched. The cutting plane is shown in the front view as the vertical line through the center. The arrows pointing to the left show that the viewer is looking in that direction.

Figure 5-12 illustrates four common hatch patterns. The upper two patterns are user-defined patterns, and the lower two are from AutoCAD's set of stored patterns. Each pattern in the figure is labeled with the name of the pattern, the scale or spacing, and the angle of the pattern. It is good practice to place hatch patterns on a separate layer. The layer can be frozen to remove its data from the regeneration that takes place from time to time.

Figure 5-12
**Common Hatch
Patterns**

User-defined pattern
45°, Spacing=0.5

User-defined pattern
60°, Spacing=0.25
Double Hatch

Stored pattern: BRASS
135°, Scale=1.0

Stored pattern: BOX
45°, Scale=1.0

To start the Hatch command, select the Hatch button from the Draw toolbar. The Boundary Hatch dialog box shown in Figure 5-13 appears. You use this dialog box to select the hatch pattern, define the area to be hatched, preview your selections, and, if you are satisfied with the results, apply the hatch pattern to the drawing.

Figure 5-13
**Boundary Hatch
Dialog Box**

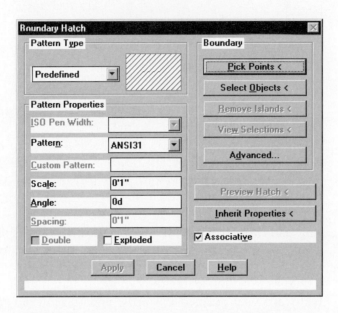

You use the options in the dialog box either to create a user-defined pattern or to select one of AutoCAD's standard patterns. To create a user-defined pattern, select User-Defined from the Pattern Type list box. Then choose the scale, angle, and spacing of the hatch lines by clicking the appropriate box and typing the desired value. You can also choose to *double hatch* the area, adding another set of lines at a 90-degree angle to the first set by clicking the Double button in the dialog box.

AutoCAD has an extensive list of stored hatch patterns that you can use just as easily as a user-defined pattern. Select the name of the pattern you want in the Pattern list box. When you select a hatch pattern by name, a sample is displayed in the Pattern Type preview box.

Use the Scale box to choose a scale for the hatch pattern. Normally you use the default scale of 1, but if the pattern is too large or too small, you can adjust the scale after you preview the hatch pattern. (Previewing is discussed later in this section.)

Now you are ready to define the boundaries of the hatched area, which must be a closed area. Click the Pick Points button in the Boundary Hatch dialog box. The prompt

    Select internal point

appears. Pick a point anywhere within a closed boundary. The message

    Analyzing internal islands

appears while AutoCAD locates the boundary. The prompt

```
Select internal point
```

reappears so you can define another boundary if you need to. Press (ENTER) if the boundary is acceptable, and you return to the Boundary Hatch dialog box. Sometimes you may have difficulty selecting an island for hatching if some of the lines are nonintersecting. You can then click the Select Objects button in the Boundary Hatch dialog box to select the objects individually that define the area for hatching.

You have selected a pattern and defined the boundary of the area to be hatched. Before you add the hatch pattern to the drawing, you can click the Preview Hatch button in the Boundary Hatch dialog box to preview the result. The hatched area is shown on the drawing. Select Continue from the Boundary Hatch box which appears. If you are satisfied with the results of your selections, click on the Apply box. If you are not satisfied, return to the Boundary Hatch dialog box and change your selections.

So far we have discussed applying hatch patterns to single closed boundaries. Figure 5-14 illustrates a situation in which you need to hatch the spaces between *nested boundaries*. To create nested hatch patterns, click the Advanced button in the Boundary Hatch dialog box. The Advanced Options dialog box opens providing three hatching styles: Normal, Outer, and Ignore. The Normal option hatches the areas between alternate sets of nested boundaries. The Outer option hatches only the area between the outer boundary and the next inner boundary. The Ignore option hatches the entire area defined by the outer boundary, ignoring all other internal boundaries. Select the hatching style by selecting the appropriate option from the three Hatching Style buttons in the Advanced Options dialog box. The icon in the upper-right corner of the dialog box changes to illustrate the effect of your choice.

To hatch within nested boundaries, click the Pick Points button in the Boundary Hatch dialog box and select points near the individual boundaries. For example, you would pick the points 1, 2, and 3 in order, as in Figure 5-14. Be careful, however, to pick points near the individual boundaries. For example, if you pick point 2 too close to the circle, AutoCAD looks inward and notes that you have already selected that boundary.

Figure 5-14
**Hatching with Nested
Boundaries**

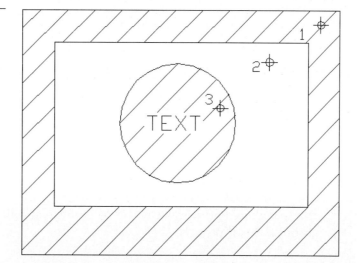

You can also have the hatch pattern skip around any text within the boundary. Before you select any of the boundaries using the Pick Points button in the Boundary Hatch dialog box, click the Select Objects button, and then click on the text you want to skip. The text is identified as a boundary and is skipped if you are using the Standard text style.

Try It

For this exercise you will construct the main part of the drawing of the approach. When you are finished, your drawing should look like that shown below.

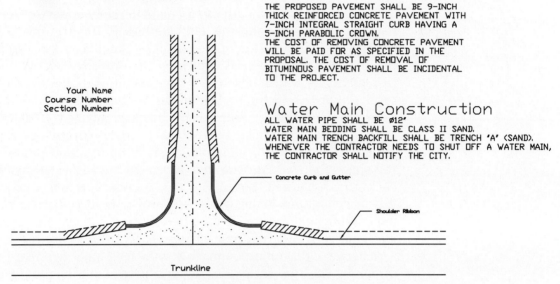

THE PROPOSED PAVEMENT SHALL BE 9-INCH
THICK REINFORCED CONCRETE PAVEMENT WITH
7-INCH INTEGRAL STRAIGHT CURB HAVING A
5-INCH PARABOLIC CROWN.
THE COST OF REMOVING CONCRETE PAVEMENT
WILL BE PAID FOR AS SPECIFIED IN THE
PROPOSAL. THE COST OF REMOVAL OF
BITUMINOUS PAVEMENT SHALL BE INCIDENTAL
TO THE PROJECT.

Water Main Construction
ALL WATER PIPE SHALL BE Ø12"
WATER MAIN BEDDING SHALL BE CLASS II SAND.
WATER MAIN TRENCH BACKFILL SHALL BE TRENCH 'A' (SAND).
WHENEVER THE CONTRACTOR NEEDS TO SHUT OFF A WATER MAIN,
THE CONTRACTOR SHALL NOTIFY THE CITY.

Your Name
Course Number
Section Number

Concrete Curb and Gutter

Shoulder Ribbon

Trunkline

Typical Approach Treatment Detail 1

◆ You will begin by drawing the two main horizontal lines for the trunkline. Draw a line from a point on the lower left of the drawing to a point @350',0 (make sure to include the ' so the distance is measured in feet). Offset the line 24' upwards and then again 28' to obtain the opposite edge of the road and the shoulder border.

◆ You will first draw the left half of the approach and then mirror it to obtain the right half. It will probably be easiest if you zoom the area on the left portion of the drawing. Draw a series of lines starting at a convenient point on the shoulder ribbon (use the NEArest Osnap mode) to a point that is @50',8' and then to @0,1.5' and finally to @10',0.

◆ Using the Start End Radius option draw an arc that begins at the endpoint of the line just created, which ends @30',30', and that has a radius of 30'.

◆ Draw the remaining lines for the left side of the approach roadway by drawing from the end of the arc just created to @0,20' and then to @3',25' and finally to @0,75'.

◆ Offset the last vertical line just drawn by 12' to the right (now you have a center line for the approach road), and then mirror the lines and curves drawn for the left half of the approach road about this center line. Extend the center line of the approach road down to the border of the trunkline, and trim away the part of the shoulder ribbon that goes through the approach.

◆ To create the curb and gutter, zoom the area surrounding the arc on the left. Offset the arc and the short vertical and horizontal lines extending from it 12″ to the left and then again 12″ from this new copy. Repeat this for the right curved section. Draw horizontal and vertical lines at the ends of the curb and gutter constructions. Select a hatch pattern of ANSI31 and a scale of 30. Make sure to preview your hatch pattern before you apply it.

◆ Add the crosshatching for the shoulders by offsetting lines 6′ from the originals. To have a well-defined boundary for crosshatching, you will have to create lines at the ends of the regions that will be removed after the hatching is added. You may need to define some of the areas for crosshatching by selecting objects rather than by picking points. Use a scale of 300 for this crosshatching.

◆ Add the crosshatching for the approach road using the AR-SAND pattern with a scale factor of 75. This will probably work best if you first sketch an outline on the drawing to be filled that you can erase after the hatching is added.

◆ Delete all of the construction lines that you added to aid in the crosshatching. Make sure you do not accidentally delete the crosshatching. If you do, select Undo to restore it. You will probably have to zoom in on portions of the drawing to be able to do this.

◆ Convert the necessary lines to center lines and to hidden lines with a scale of 400. Your drawing should now look like the one shown in the figure (although your drawing will not include the labels).

5-3 ENTERING POINTS ON AN OBJECT

The Measure and Divide commands enter points equally spaced along a line or a curve. These points are nodes that you can use in later editing problems. The Measure command starts from one end of the object and marks off equal distances along the object. Any leftover segment less than the specified segment length is found at the other end of the object. The Divide command divides an object into a specified number of equal-length segments and inserts points at the division points. Figure 5-15 compares identical arcs with points inserted using the Measure and Divide commands.

Figure 5-15
Comparing Measure and Divide

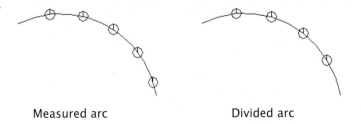

Measured arc   Divided arc

Using the Measure and Divide Commands

To issue the Measure command, point to the Point button on the Draw toolbar, press the left button on the mouse, and select Measure from the resulting graphical pop-up menu. At the prompt

```
Select object to measure:
```

pick a single object near the end from which the measuring is to begin. At the next prompt

```
<Segment length>/Block:
```

enter a numerical distance. AutoCAD enters point symbols along the object using the current Point Mode and Point Size settings. The Block option allows you to use a symbol of your own creation to mark the points.

Before you start the Divide command, you must make sure that the Point Style and Point Size settings are made (refer to Chapter 3 if you need to). To start the Divide command, choose the Divide button on the Point graphical pop-up menu. At the prompt

```
Select object to divide.
```

Pick a single object. At the prompt

```
<Number of segments>/Block:
```

enter the integer that represents the number of segments you want the object divided into. Again, the Block option allows you to use a symbol of your own creation to mark the points.

5-4   ADDING DIMENSIONS TO YOUR DRAWINGS

Dimensions are an essential part of most engineering drawings. While some of the schematic drawings that you have seen so far have not required dimensions, drawings of objects or facilities that are going to be manufactured or constructed must be completely dimensioned. You use dimensions to show the length of lines, the radius of arcs and circles, and the angles between lines. While most dimensions use only numerical values, some dimensions combine text with numerical data. It is good practice to place dimensions on a separate layer in a contrasting color so they are easy to identify.

The AutoCAD Dimensioning commands automatically draw the lines, arcs, and arrowheads that make up the body of a dimension. In addition, AutoCAD calculates the lengths and angles that are being dimensioned and adds the appropriate text to the dimension. The AutoCAD Dimensioning commands let you control dimension features, such as the arrowhead style and the alignment and height of the text.

Figure 5-16 illustrates the basic components of standard linear and angular dimensions. The components of a *linear dimension* consist of the *dimension line*, the *extension line*, the *dimension arrow*, and the *dimension text*. The extension line extends from a point on the object to a point slightly beyond the dimension line. *Angular dimensions* have the same components but use arcs as dimension lines. The extension lines radiate from the origin of the angle being measured.

Figure 5-16
**Basic Dimensioning
Components**

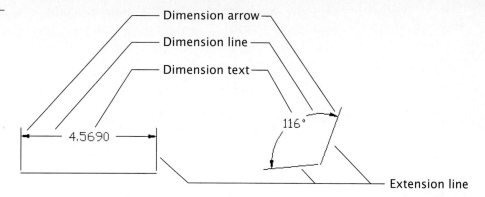

In general, to add dimensions you first select the type of dimension, points on the object, and the location of the dimension line and text. AutoCAD then calculates the distance involved and enters the text along with the components of the dimension.

All of the Dimensioning commands are found on the Dimensioning toolbar shown in Figure 5-17. To display this toolbar, choose **Toolbars** from the **Tools** pull-down menu, and then choose **Dimensioning** from the next menu that appears. Note that the buttons on the toolbar may not have the exact same arrangement as shown in the figure, but it should look essentially the same. The Dimensioning command options of Linear, Angular, and Radius are discussed in this section.

Figure 5-17
Dimensioning Toolbar

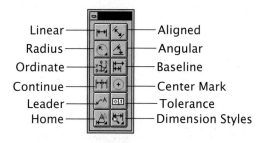

Using Linear Dimensions

Linear dimensions include horizontal, vertical, aligned, and rotated dimensions, which are illustrated in Figure 5-18. Horizontal and vertical dimensions are illustrated on the left side of the figure. The aligned dimension measures the true length of the line and is parallel to the line. The rotated dimension measures the length of the line, projected in a direction that is not perpendicular to the line. The 1.00 dimension in Figure 5-18 is the distance between the ends of the vertical line, projected at an angle of 45 degrees from the horizontal axis.

Figure 5-18
**Linear Dimension
Options**

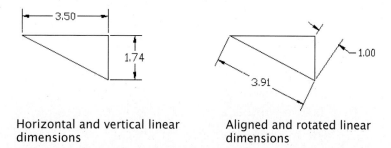

Horizontal and vertical linear   Aligned and rotated linear
dimensions   dimensions

Click the Linear button on the Dimensioning toolbar. The prompts and responses for three of the Linear dimensioning options—Horizontal, Vertical, and Aligned—are identical. You are prompted for the origins of the extension lines, the location of the dimension line, and the dimension text. At the prompt

```
First extension line origin or RETURN to select:
```

pick a point at one end of the line you are dimensioning. At the prompt

```
Second extension line origin:
```

pick the other end of the line. AutoCAD then guesses which type of linear dimension you wish to add to your drawing. At the prompt

```
Dimension line location (Text/Angle/Horizontal/Vertical/
Rotated):
```

either pick a point to locate the dimension line if AutoCAD has guessed correctly or choose an option to indicate that you have a different type of dimension that AutoCAD guessed. The dimension and the text move as you move the crosshairs to help you position the dimension line. The default dimension text is the length of the line. You can modify the text or substitute different text if necessary, as discussed later in the chapter.

When you click the Linear button on the Dimensioning toolbar, and then choose the Rotated option, AutoCAD presents the prompt

```
Dimension line angle <0d>:
```

Enter the angle the dimension line is to make with the positive X axis. The zero angle is the equivalent to measuring the horizontal distance between the length of the lines. A response of 90 degrees measures the vertical length of the line. After you enter the angle, the remaining prompts and responses are the same as for the previous linear dimensions.

The Dimensioning toolbar shown in Figure 5-17 includes two other commonly used buttons for linear dimensions: Continue and Baseline. The Continue button allows you to dimension a second line that is a continuation of the first dimension line. The top dimensions in Figure 5-19, 1.50 and 2.50, were entered using the Continue option. The Baseline button allows you to dimension a second line but uses the origin of the first extension line for both dimensions. The dimensions 2.00 and 4.00 were entered using the Baseline option.

Figure 5-19
**Continue and Baseline
Options**

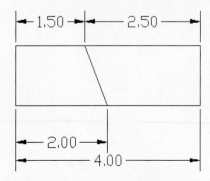

To use either of these options, initiate the Linear command to create the first dimension, but instead of creating a second linear dimension, click either the Baseline or the Continue button. At the prompt

```
Second extension line origin or RETURN to select:
```

pick the location of the second extension line. AutoCAD uses a prior extension line as the first extension line and completes the dimension. The location of the second dimension line is determined by AutoCAD based on the option being used. You may have to move some of the individual dimensions around on the drawing when you are finished to make sure that they appear correctly.

Using Angular Dimensions

The Angular button on the Dimensioning toolbar measures the angle between two nonparallel lines and displays the value in degrees. Dimensioning angles is just as easy as dimensioning linear objects. The dimension line component of an angular dimension consists of an arc. Generally you will be dimensioning an angle defined by two lines in a drawing. However, the Angular option will dimension the angle defined by the endpoints of an arc or by two points that you select on a circle. After you choose the method for defining the angle, you select one of four locations for the dimension arc. Two of these locations are illustrated by the dimensions at point B in Figure 5-20. Each of the angles is possible depending on where you choose to place the dimension arc. Finally, you select the point where you will enter the dimension text. If the point you choose causes the arc to intersect the text, the arc is broken.

Figure 5-20
Angular Dimensions

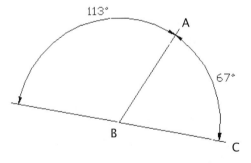

Here are the prompts and responses for angular dimensions. Click the Angular button on the Dimensioning toolbar. The first prompt is

```
Select arc, circle, line, or RETURN:
```

Pick the first line that defines the angle. At the prompt

```
Second line:
```

pick the second line that defines the angle. The prompt

```
Dimension arc line location (Text/Angle):
```

appears. AutoCAD shows you the dimension arc and the text. You drag the dimension arc and text as you move the crosshairs. When you are satisfied with the location, pick the point. The dimension is now located on the drawing at the point you specified.

At the prompt

```
Select arc, circle, line, or RETURN:
```

press (ENTER) to select the Return option. You can then select the intersection of the two lines that contain the angle and are not required to select the two lines separately. After that the command proceeds as before.

You can use the Angular option to dimension the central angle defined by the endpoints of an arc or by any two points on the perimeter of a circle. Figure 5-21 illustrates the central angles defined by an arc and two points on a circle. Notice that no radial lines are needed to define the angle.

Figure 5-21
Dimensioning Central Angles

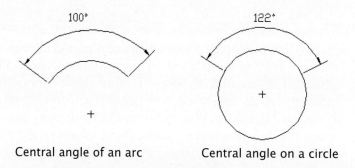

Central angle of an arc   Central angle on a circle

If you pick an arc at the prompt,

```
Select arc, circle, line, or RETURN:
```

AutoCAD displays the prompt

```
Dimension arc line location (Text/Angle):
```

All you have to do is select the location for the dimension arc and proceed as before. When you pick a point on the circumference of a circle, the prompt

```
Second angle point:
```

appears. Pick another point on the circle and the usual prompts appear until the dimension is complete. The center of the arc or circle is the origin of the lines defining the angle. In the case of the arc, the angle is defined by the center of the arc and the ends of the arc. In the case of the circle, the center and the two points on the perimeter define the angle. After you define the angle, the command proceeds as before.

Using Radial Dimensions

You use the Radial button on the Dimensioning toolbar to enter radial or diametral dimensions: the radius or the diameter of an arc or circle. The results of the Diameter and Radius options are illustrated in Figure 5-22.

Figure 5-22
Radial Dimensions

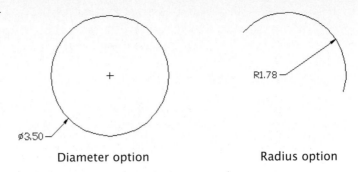

Diameter option   Radius option

Use the Diameter option to dimension circles, and use the Radius option for both arcs and circles. Both options require you to select the arc or circle. The dimension line, or leader, is a radial line through the point that you pick on the circumference of the arc or circle (leaders are described in more detail in the next section). AutoCAD calculates the radius or diameter and enters it on the dimension line. The dimension is placed outside, and a leader is extended to the text. A circle symbol is added to diameter dimensions, and the letter R is added to radius dimensions. Center marks are added to the figure by default.

When you point to the Radius button on the Dimensioning toolbar, hold the mouse button down and then select the Diameter button on the resulting graphical pop-up menu, the prompt

```
Select arc or circle:
```

appears. Select an arc or circle, and the prompt

```
Dimension line location<Text/Angle>:
```

appears. When you move the crosshairs, the dimension and the leader move to help you pick the location for the dimension. The dimension is entered with a pair of lines pointing to the circle. These lines make up the leader.

The prompts for the Radius option are nearly identical to those for Diameter.

Using Leaders

The leader is a very useful dimensioning tool that allows you to point to an object and describe it with a note. The Radius and Diameter commands use leaders automatically. You can also create leaders by selecting the Leader button from the Dimensioning toolbar. First you are prompted to draw the lines that make up the leader. The first line segment is at an angle from the object and displays an arrow pointing to the start point. The second line is a short horizontal segment. After drawing the lines, you are prompted for the text. Leaders are illustrated in Figure 5-23.

Figure 5-23
**Using Leaders and
Appending Text**

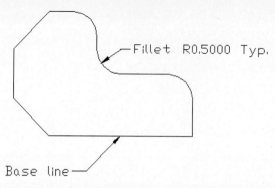

When you start the Leader command, the first prompt is

    From point:

Pick a point near where you want the tip of the arrow to appear. At the prompt

    To point:

pick a point at the end of the first angled leader line. The prompt

    To point (Format/Annotation/Undo)<Annotation>:

continues to appear until you press ⓔⓝⓣⓔⓡ without picking a point. At the next prompt

    Annotation (or RETURN for options):

type the first line of the note. The next prompt will be

    MText:

Either type the second line of the note or press ⓔⓝⓣⓔⓡ again to finish the note.

Adding Text to Dimensions

At times you will want to add text of your own to the default dimension text. For example, to indicate that a certain dimension is typical of others on the drawing, you can add the note "Typical" before the contents of the default text. At the

    Dimension type of dimension (Text/Angle):

prompt that AutoCAD displays during the course of any dimensioning command, type T and press ⓔⓝⓣⓔⓡ to select the Text option. The Edit MText dialog box appears. The dimension value is signified by brackets in this dialog box (<>) and you can edit the text to include words such as *Typical* either before or after these brackets. In fact, you can enter notes before and after the default dimension text by typing the first part of the note before the <> and then typing the second part. Typing the text in this order places the default dimension text between the two parts of the note.

This technique was used to enter the dimension and note "Fillet R0.5000 Typ." shown in Figure 5-23.

Setting Dimension Styles

To create a drawing with clear and legible dimensions, most of the time you will need to edit the default dimension settings to account for things like the size of the model space. If you click the Dimension Styles button from the Dimensioning toolbar, the Dimension Styles dialog box shown in Figure 5-24 appears.

Figure 5-24
Dimension Styles Dialog Box

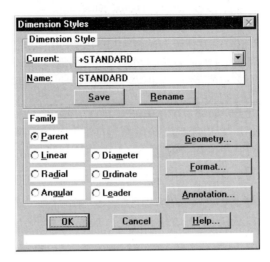

If you click the Geometry button in this dialog box, a new dialog box appears. From this new dialog box you are able to set the size of arrowheads and control such things as the length of the extension and dimension lines as well as the center marks for arcs and circles. If you click the Format button in the Dimension Styles dialog box, you can specify the orientation of the text within the dimension lines. For example, you can specify whether or not the text is in the middle of the dimension line or is above or below it. If you click the Annotation button in the Dimension Styles dialog box, you can change the characteristics of the dimension text, including the size of the gap, the text height and the units displayed in the dimensions. It is best to set the dimension style correctly before you begin dimensioning your drawing, because once you specify a dimension style, then all subsequent dimensions will be created using that style.

Editing Dimensions

You may want to modify dimensions after you add them to a drawing. The components of the dimension are created as a combined entity, similar to a block. You can edit a dimension by choosing **Properties** from the **Edit** pull-down menu and then selecting the dimension to be changed. You are presented with a dialog box that contains similar options to those found on the Dimension Styles dialog box for editing the dimension. To customize a specific dimension, you may find it easier to explode the dimension so that you can modify individual pieces of it. However, great care should be taken before you explode any dimensions. It is always best to edit your dimensions using the dimension editing commands whenever possible.

Figure 5-27
Detail A

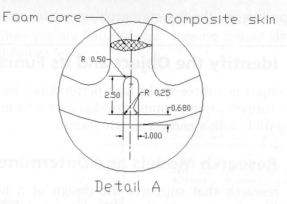

Detail A

 4. Make Appropriate Screen Adjustments

Set up another prototype drawing. Set the limits so that the drawing of the wheel and the detail fit on the screen. Use decimal units with three decimal places. Set up separate layers for the continuous and hidden lines. Set up a layer for the dimensions and notes. Use a contrasting color for the dimension layer.

 5. Draw, Print or Plot, and Save the File

A suggested order in which to draw the components of the wheel was outlined in step 3. You should plan the location of the dimensions so that they are clear. You also need to develop a plan for drawing the detail shown in Figure 5-27, both as an enlarged drawing and on the wheel drawing. Save the drawing as WHEEL.

What If **What if the wheel had four spokes? Would this require any major change in the drawing process?**

What if you knew the thickness of the spoke? Could you use the thickness and the width of the spoke and draw an approximation to the section shown in Figure 5-27? Could you use a combination of an ellipse and several arcs to draw the approximation?

SUMMARY   In this chapter you learned to add annotation to your drawing. The primary types of drawing annotation are text, hatching and dimensions. You also learned how to use the Measure and Divide commands to enter points along objects.

Key Words

angular dimension	hatch pattern
control code	leader
diametral dimension	linear dimension
dimension arrow	nested boundaries
dimension line	radial dimensions
dimension text	rotation angle
double hatch	title block
extension line	

Exercises

Draw the objects shown in the following exercises. Use the dimensions where given. Draw the schematic approximately to scale. Add dimensions and notes where they are supplied.

Exercise 5-1
Border and Title Block

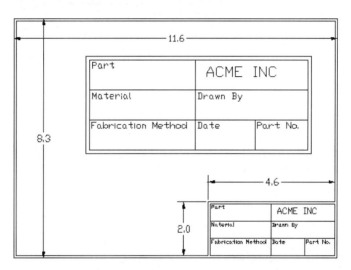

a. Add the Border and Title Block to each of your prototype drawings as shown in Exercise 5-1.
b. Put your name in the Drawn By area.

Exercise 5-2
Angle Bracket

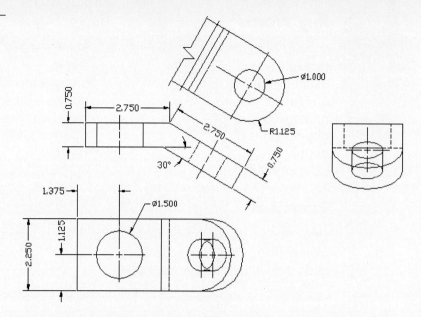

Draw the four views of the bracket. Note the use of ellipses to represent the circles as they appear in the right and lower views.

Exercise 5-3
Wide Flange Column Base Plate

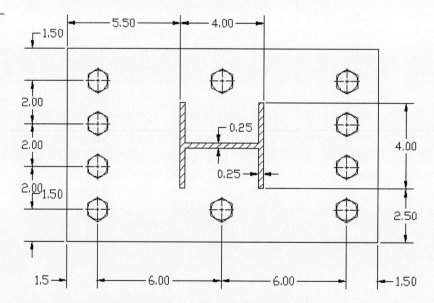

a. Use the block of the hexagonal bolt head.
b. Array the bolt heads and erase the extra ones.
c. Add dimensions to your drawing.

Exercise 5-4
Casting

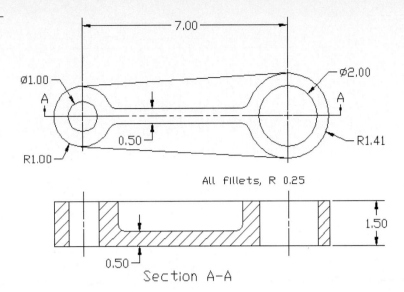

All fillets, R 0.25

Section A-A

Exercise 5-5A
Gear

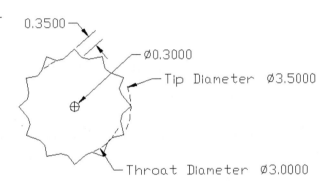

Exercise 5-5B
Tooth Detail

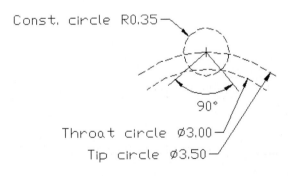

a. Draw one tooth using the dimensions shown in the detail.
b. Use the Array command to complete the gear.
c. Add dimensions to your drawing.

Exercise 5-6
Fin Plate

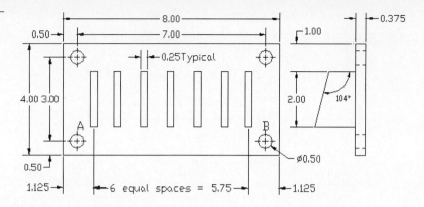

Exercise 5-7
Landscape Design

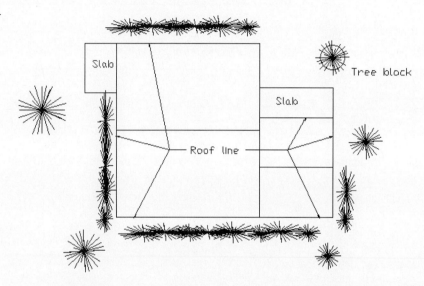

a. Open the drawing of the Foundation Plan you created in Chapter 3, Exercise 3-6.
b. Draw the roof lines two feet beyond the foundation walls.
c. Draw a tree symbol using radial lines emanating from the center of a circle, similar to the Tree block shown.
d. Make a block, without the circle, and insert it into the drawing to simulate trees and the plantings along the building.

6 Making Three-Dimensional Drawings

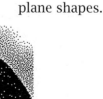

Finite Element Analysis Engineers use curved surfaces in a great variety of modern structures. Radio telescopes, modern aircraft bodies, curved roofs, and high-performance bicycle wheels are all examples of curved surfaces. To analyze the surfaces of such complex objects, engineers use a numerical technique called finite element analysis. Finite element analysis yields very accurate data about the structural behavior of the actual curved surface. CAD systems are used to make the 3D models of the surface. The results are then used in the numerical analysis. In this chapter you will draw a roof structure that consists of a hyperbolic paraboloid—a means of constructing "curved" surfaces from plane shapes.

INTRODUCTION

All of the drawings in the previous chapters have been two dimensional (2D)—that is, the Z coordinate of each point is zero. This chapter introduces some techniques for drawing *three-dimensional* (*3D*) objects, objects that have *thickness* in the Z direction. The first techniques involve creating a 3D object from a 2D object. When you add thickness to a two-dimensional object, the 3D drawing that results is called an *extruded object.* You can also revolve a 2D figure about an axis to form a 3D object. After you've learned to create 3D objects, you learn how to view the drawings so the objects appear in three dimensions. You then learn how to create *primitives*—boxes, cylinders, cones, and spheres. You can combine two 3D objects to form a third object by subtracting, adding (union) or intersecting. Another technique for drawing 3D objects is to draw the outlines of the object using Z coordinates along with X and Y coordinates. These 3D drawings are called *wireframe models*, or simply *wireframes.* As you draw wireframes, you learn how to create and use custom coordinate systems. So far you have been drawing in the default or World Coordinate System. You must be able to create custom or User Coordinate Systems to edit successfully in three dimensions. At the end of this chapter, you learn how to combine views of a 3D drawing into a set of orthographic views that are suitable for engineering purposes.

6-1   CREATING EXTRUDED OR REVOLVED 3D OBJECTS

You are already familiar with everyday items that can be drawn easily as extruded or revolved objects. A cylinder is formed by revolving a rectangle along one of its edges. A rectangular box, or prism, is formed by extruding a rectangle along a line perpendicular to the plane of the rectangle. Figure 6-1 illustrates the 3D objects formed by revolving or by extruding a rectangle (the rectangle appears distorted because of the 3D viewpoint).

Figure 6-1
**Revolved and
Extruded Rectangles**

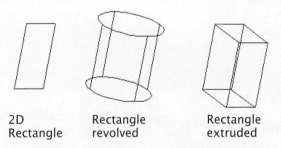

2D   Rectangle   Rectangle
Rectangle   revolved   extruded

To create 3D objects in AutoCAD you use the Solids toolbar shown in Figure 6-2. Display this toolbar by selecting **Toolbars** from the **Tools** pulldown menu and then selecting **Solids** from the subsequent menu. A tool bar similar to the one shown in Figure 6-2 appears. The buttons on your Solids toolbar may be arranged differently than those shown in the figure.

Figure 6-2
Solids Toolbar

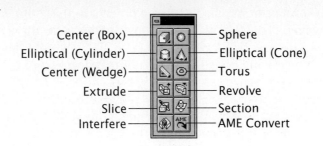

To extrude a 2D figure, first draw the figure and then select the Extrude button on the Solids toolbar. At the prompt

```
Select objects:
```

pick the objects to be extruded. At the prompt

```
Path/<Height of Extrusion>:
```

enter the extrusion distance (the dimension perpendicular to the plane of the 2D figure) and press (ENTER). At the prompt

```
Extrusion taper angle <0>:
```

press (ENTER) to accept the default value of zero or enter a value for the loft (taper) of the 3D part.

To revolve a 2D figure, first draw the figure and then select the Revolve button on the Solids toolbar. At the prompt

```
Select objects:
```

pick the objects to be revolved. At the prompt

```
Axis of Revolution-Object/X/Y/<Start point of axis>:
```

select the first point that defines the axis of revolution (you can use one of the Osnap modes for this). At the prompt

```
<End point of axis>:
```

select the second point that defines the axis of revolution. At the prompt

```
Angle of revolution <full circle>:
```

enter an angular value for the revolution or press (ENTER) to accept the default of a full circle.

6-2   VIEWING OPTIONS IN 3D

When you revolve or extrude a 2D figure, your 3D object does not initially appear to be three dimensional. You need to change the viewpoint or orientation of the XYZ coordinate system relative to the viewer. AutoCAD has several options for displaying objects in three dimensions all of which are available on the View pull-down menu. The three most commonly used options are 3D Viewpoint Presets, 3D Viewpoint, and 3D Dynamic View.

When you choose **3D Viewpoint Presets** from the **View** menu, a second menu appears that allows you to choose any of several pre-established views. In particular, you can choose one of the principal orthographic views (top, front, right side, and so on), a plan view of the object, or one of four different isometric views. When you choose **3D Viewpoint** from the **View** menu, a second menu appears with three options on it. The Vector option offers the easiest method for establishing a view. In the default orientation of the axes, you (the viewer) are looking along the Z axis down on to the XY plane; thus your point of view is located at a vector of 0,0,1 (you are standing along the Z axis and looking back at the origin). The vector orientation of an isometric view is 1,1,1 and the vector location of the top view is 0,1,0, and so on. Figure 6-3 shows a cylinder from three different 3D viewpoints.

Figure 6-3
3D View Vectors

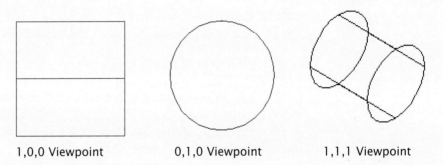

1,0,0 Viewpoint   0,1,0 Viewpoint   1,1,1 Viewpoint

A third way to change your viewpoint is to choose **3D Dynamic View** from the **View** pull-down menu. You will be prompted to select the objects for dynamic viewing. After selecting the objects, you can click a point on the drawing and move the mouse around on the mouse pad. As you move the mouse, the objects rotate in 3D space and follow the mouse pointer until you click again. You can reset the 3D view of the objects several times in this manner before finalizing your choice by pressing (ENTER).

Try It   In this exercise you will create two different 3D objects and then experiment with some of the 3D viewing options.

◆ Start a new drawing. You will begin by drawing two different 2D figures. For the first figure draw a polyline *from* a point in the lower-left part of the screen to @1,0, *to* @0,.5, to @–.25,1.5, to @–.75,0 and then back to the original point of the figure. Zoom the figure so that it nearly fills the screen. Create a fillet in the upper-right corner of the figure, which has a radius of 0.25. For the second 2D figure create a polyline *from* a convenient point located *to* the right of the figure just drawn to @4,–1.25, to @4,1.25, to @–4,1.25 and then back to the orginal point on the figure. You should now have a diamond shaped figure on the screen. Create fillets of radius 0.5 at the left and right corners of the figure, and create fillets of radius 1.0 at the top and bottom corners of the figure.

◆ Display the Solids toolbar, and revolve the first 2D figure you drew to form a solid. The axis of revolution should be the line defined by the vertical left side of the figure, and the angle of revolution should be a full circle.

◆ Extrude the second figure you drew a distance of 0.5 without specifying a taper.

◆ Experiment with various 3D viewing options. In particular, you may wish to use some of the preset views or the dynamic viewing options. The 3D objects you have created should look similar to the ones shown in the figure below.

 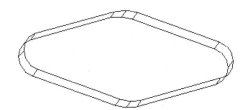

6-3   CREATING PRIMITIVES

When creating solid objects it is often convenient to create primitives such as boxes, cones, cylinders, and spheres. AutoCAD has two primitives that are unique—the torus and the wedge. You could create all of the primitive shapes by either extrusion or revolution, so it may seem to you that their inclusion is redundant. However, often you can save time by directly creating a box of the appropriate dimensions rather than drawing a rectangle and then extruding it to form a box.

When creating a primitive shape, you must specify certain features. For example, if you are creating a sphere, you must specify the location of the center of the sphere and its radius. Once AutoCAD has this information, it can create the sphere with the appropriate size and in the proper location. Similarly, you create cylinders by locating the center of one circular base, the radius of the circle and the center of the opposite circular end (this defines the height of the cylinder). Elliptical cylinders are defined in much the same way, except that the elliptical cross-section requires more than just a center and a single radius to define it.

To create a box by using the Center option you first select the Center (Box) button from the Solids toolbar. At the prompt

        Center of box <0,0,0>:

you either type the coordinates of the desired center of one of the faces of the box and press (ENTER), or you can pick a point on the screen by using the mouse. At the prompt

        Cube/Length/<corner of box>:

you select a point located at one of the corner points for the face of the box, and at the prompt

    Height:

you enter the height of the box in a direction perpendicular to the face of the box you previously defined. Note that this is similar to creating a rectangle and then extruding it, but that all of the steps are combined in one operation instead of two.

    You follow similar procedures to create the other available primitives in AutoCAD.

6-4 COMBINING SOLID OBJECTS

You have learned how to create individual extruded, revolved, and primitive objects and how to view them in three dimensions. Now you will learn how to combine two 3D objects to create a third more complicated object. Figure 6-4 shows an object you cannot create by any of the methods you have learned up to this point. However, it does look as if you could create a cylinder (either by extrusion, revolution, or as a primitive) and then combine it with a box. This box with a circular cylinder on top resembles a column on a pedestal. The left image in the figure shows how the object looks from the default point of view. The right image shows how the object appears in three dimensions.

Figure 6-4
Column–Pedestal Object

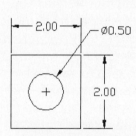
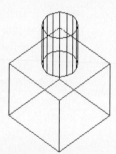

    To combine 3D objects, you can use either the Union, Subtract or Intersect options found on the graphical pop-up menu displayed when you point to the Explode button on the Modify toolbar. You must first create the two different objects for combining, and then you must make sure that they are properly located in space relative to one another. In general, two objects must interfere, or overlap, before you can combine them. Sometimes the objects can be just touching, but most of the time you will want the two objects to overlap.

    When you combine the two objects using the Union command, the overlapping volume is absorbed into the new object, and the resulting object contains the outline of the two original objects. When you subtract two objects, you must define the object to subtract from and the object that will do the subtracting. The resulting object consists of the original object to be subtracted from minus any overlapping volume with the subtracting object. When you intersect two objects, the resulting object is just the overlapping volume that existed between the two original objects.

Figure 6-5 shows a cone and a cylinder and the various results which are obtained by combining these two objects.

Figure 6-5
Combining Objects

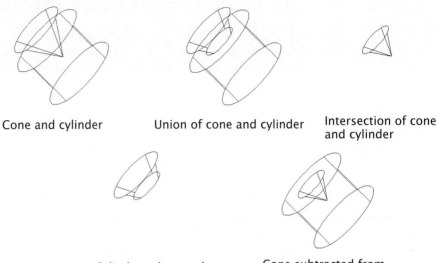

Cone and cylinder   Union of cone and cylinder   Intersection of cone and cylinder

Cylinder subtracted from cone   Cone subtracted from cylinder

6-5   ORIENTING SOLID OBJECTS

Before you combine solid objects, you may need to move them to their proper location in space. In particular, you should orient the objects so that they are overlapping or interfering. In Chapter 3 you learned how to move and rotate 2D objects. To move and rotate 3D objects, you follow a similar procedure.

To move a 3D object you click the Move button on the Modify toolbar. When prompted for the first and second points of the displacement, you input a point that is defined by X, Y, and Z coordinates. Previously, you moved objects by an X and Y translation only—the Z coordinates of the translation vectors defaulted to zero.

Rotating an object in 3D is a little bit more complicated than rotating in 2D. When you rotate a 2D object, you always rotate about the Z axis, which is perpendicular to the plane of the computer screen and pointing out towards you. A counterclockwise rotation is a positive rotation about the Z axis and a negative rotation is a clockwise rotation about the Z axis as you look down the positive Z axis. Similarly, a rotation of a 3D solid about the Y axis is made as if you are looking down the Y axis and rotating the object in a counterclockwise manner and a positive X rotation is made as if you are looking down the X axis and rotating the object in a counter- clockwise manner. As you rotate objects you supply the rotation pivot point, the line of rotation, and the angular amount of rotation.

To rotate an object in 3D, point to the Rotate button on the Modify tool- bar, hold down the pick button on the mouse and select the 3D Rotate button on the resulting graphical pop-up menu. At the

```
Select Objects:
```

prompt, select the objects you wish to orient and press (ENTER). At the next prompt

> `Axis by Object/Last/View/Xaxis/Yaxis/Zaxis/<2points>:`

you must supply the line about which the object should be rotated. The most common rotation axes are the X, Y, or Z axes. Type either X, Y, or Z at the prompt as appropriate, and press (ENTER). At the prompt

> `Point on axis <0,0,0>:`

enter the coordinates of the pivot point on the axis. Usually, the origin (0,0,0) is sufficient. At the prompt

> `<Rotation Angle>/Reference:`

type the angular value for the rotation and press (ENTER). The 3D object will be relocated in space appropriately. When making 3D rotations, you will probably want to observe the screen icon which may be hidden by the Modify toolbar depending on your default screen layout. To view the icon, drag the Modify toolbar to a different location on the screen before proceeding with the object rotation. Figure 6-6 shows an object that has been rotated about the X, Y, and Z axes for comparison purposes.

Figure 6-6
Rotating Objects in 3 Dimensions

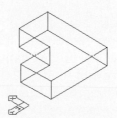

Original object position

Original object rotated about X axis

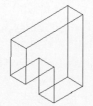

Original object rotated about Y axis

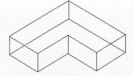

Original object rotated about Z axis

Try It

In this exercise you will continue working with the two solids you created in the previous Try It! exercise. When you are finished your object should look similar to the one shown in the following figure.

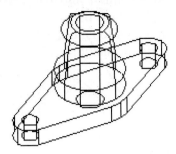

◆ Create a cylinder with a radius of 0.25 and a height of 0.5. Move the cylinder you just created so that its center coincides with the center of the arc for the piece that you extruded earlier. You can use the Osnap mode of CENter to accomplish this. Subtract the cylinder from the extruded base. Repeat this step for the hole on the other end of the extruded piece.

◆ Rotate the object that you formed by revolution in the last TryIt! exercise 90 degrees about the X axis. After you rotate the object, it may move out of view on the screen. Select Zoom All from the View pull-down menu to show the entire drawing. Move the object so that the center of the bottom circle coincides with the center of one of the small holes you just created. Move the object again by specifying the second point as @2.33,0 or @–2.33,0 to align the object in the middle of the extruded plate. Add the two parts together using the Union command.

◆ Create a cylinder with a radius of 0.4 and a height of 3 to cut a hole in the middle of this object. Note that the cylinder is longer than necessary to go all the way through the object, but after the subtraction the excess material on the subtracting object is removed.

◆ Move this object on the screen either by translating or by executing the 3D Rotate command to verify that it is one single object.

6-6   ASSEMBLING THE TOOLS TO CREATE WIREFRAMES

Sometimes you may find that you need to draw a device known as a wireframe model, or wireframe. An example of a wireframe model is shown in Figure 6-7. (You will draw this device, called an alignment block, later in this chapter.)

Wireframes in AutoCAD are similar to the physical models you can construct using wires. You draw lines and curves in three dimensions, connecting them to outline the shape of the object.

Creating a Box for a Wireframe

One strategy for drawing wireframes is to create a box that contains the device and then remove those pieces that are not part of the finished product. You need to know how to draw the box in three dimensions before you can continue. It is important to note that this is a wireframe box and not a solid primitive. A process of drawing a box involves the following steps:

Table 6-1   UCS Options

Option	Results
World	Restores the WCS.
Origin	Prompts you for an origin point. The origin of the current coordinate system, WCS or UCS, is moved to the point that you select.
Z Axis Vector	Prompts you for an origin point and a point on the positive portion of the Z axis. The positive X and Y coordinate directions are oriented according to the conventional mathematical coordinate directions.
3-Point	Prompts you, in order, for an origin point, a point on the positive X axis, and a point on the positive Y axis. The UCS is established according to these three points.
Object	Prompts you to select an object to orient the UCS. You pick a line. The origin is placed at the end of the line nearest the point you picked when selecting the line. The positive X axis is directed toward the other end of the line.
View	Creates a UCS parallel to the plane of the screen.
X Axis Rotate	Prompts you for a rotation angle about the X axis. The current UCS is rotated about the X axis by the angle that you enter.
Y Axis Rotate	Prompts you for a rotation angle about the Y axis. The current UCS is rotated about the Y axis by the angle that you enter.
Z Axis Rotate	Prompts you for a rotation angle about the Z axis. The current UCS is rotated about the Z axis by the angle that you enter.
Previous	Restores the last UCS that was used.
Save	Prompts you for a name and saves the current UCS with that name.
Restore	Prompts you for a name and makes the named UCS current.
Delete	Prompts you for the names of saved UCSs. Any UCSs that you specify are deleted and cannot be reinstated with the Restore option.
List	Lists the saved UCSs by name.

pick a point to select the direction of the positive X axis (note that the default point coordinates displayed within the brackets can vary depending on the current location of the origin). At the prompt

```
Point on the positive-Y portion of the UCS X-Y plane
<0.000,0.000,1.000>:
```

pick or enter a point to select the direction of the positive Y axis. This is illustrated in Figure 6-9.

Figure 6-9
Creating a UCS with the 3-point Option

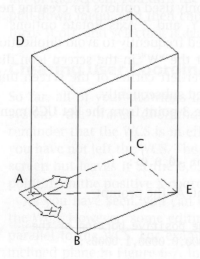

When you select **X Axis Rotate** from the **Set UCS** menu, the following prompt appears:

```
Rotation angle about the X axis <0>:
```

Enter an angle, and the current UCS system is rotated about the X axis by that amount.

When you select **Y Axis Rotate** from the **Set UCS** menu, AutoCAD displays the prompt

```
Rotation angle about the Y axis <0>:
```

Again, enter an angle, and the current UCS system is rotated about the Y axis by that amount.

Finally, when you select **Z Axis Rotate** from the **Set UCS** menu, the prompt

```
Rotation angle about the Z axis <0>:
```

appears. Enter an angle, and the current UCS system is rotated about the Z axis by that amount.

Using the rotation options to change the current UCS into a new UCS may require two rotations. Converting the UCS in Figure 6-9 to the UCS in Figure 6-10 is just such a situation. You must first rotate the UCS about the X axis to orient the Y axis from A to D; then you must rotate the UCS about the Y axis to orient the X axis from A to C. Figure 6-11 illustrates the Z axis rotate command.

Figure 6-10
Creating a UCS with the X Axis Rotate and Y Axis Rotate

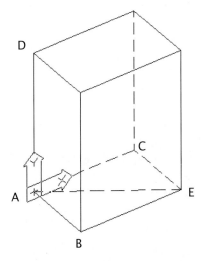

The Z axis does not appear with any of the UCS icons. Again, the direction of the Z axis is consistent with what you have learned in mathematics or physics.

Later in the chapter you will need to capture views of a 3D drawing as blocks. One of those views is the image as seen with the current viewpoint. To capture a view, you need a UCS parallel to the screen. You create the View UCS simply by selecting **View** from the **Set UCS** menu.

Figure 6-11
**Creating a UCS with
the Z Axis Rotate
Option**

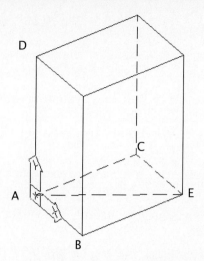

When you create a User Coordinate System, you change the location in space of the origin. However, the icon remains in the lower-left corner of the screen. To move the icon to a new origin, choose **UCS** from the **Options** pull-down menu, and then choose the **Icon Origin** option. To restore the screen icon to the lower-left corner of the screen, select this option again. However, you cannot move the icon until you first create a User Coordinate System.

Try It

In this exercise you will create a simple 3D wireframe box and then create various UCSs which are associated with the model.

◆ Draw a box similar to the one shown in Figure 6-8. Use angles of 235 degrees for the X axis and 35 degrees for the XY plane for your new viewpoint. Use the Edit Properties command to create the four dashed lines. You have drawn a simple wireframe model of the box.

◆ Create the UCS shown in Figure 6-9. Note the appearance of the UCS icon.

◆ Move the icon to the origin of the UCS.

◆ Save the UCS, using the name ABC.

◆ Create the UCS shown in Figure 6-10 starting from the UCS in Figure 6-9. Save it with the name ACD.

◆ Move the screen icon back to the lower-left corner of the screen.

◆ Make the ABC UCS current with the Restore option.

◆ Create the UCS shown in Figure 6-11. Save it with the name ABD.

◆ Experiment with the command by moving the origin of the ABD UCS to point E, and direct the X axis toward B and the Y axis toward C. Move the icon to the origin to verify your results.

◆ Restore the ABD UCS. Rotate the ABD UCS so that the positive Y direction is from A toward B and the positive X direction is downward.

◆ Use the 3point option to create the UCS in Figure 6-12. Save this UCS as AED.

◆ Create the View UCS of the object in Figure 6-12. Save the UCS as VIEW.

◆ Restore the WCS. Practice using the Previous option to recall the last UCS. Practice using the Restore option. As you change to a different UCS, note any changes to the screen icon. Restore the ABD UCS. Rotate the ABD UCS so that the positive Y direction is from A toward B and the positive X direction is downward.

◆ Save the drawing as UCSWF for use later in the chapter.

Figure 6-12
Creating a UCS on an Inclined Surface

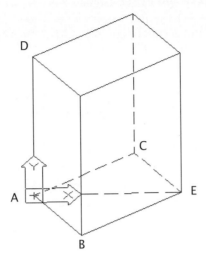

Defining Curved Surfaces

You use *ruling lines* to create *ruled surfaces* that are curved in wireframe models. When you create extrusions of curves, AutoCAD adds the ruling lines automatically. When you draw curved surfaces as wireframes, you must add ruling lines to define the curved surface.

You use the Ruled Surface command to define ruled surfaces. After initiating the command you need to pick two objects, called *defining curves*, to determine the location and orientation of the ruling lines. (Note that you cannot mix open and closed curves.) AutoCAD then divides each object into a set number of intervals and draws lines from the division points on one object to the corresponding division points on the other object. If you select an open curve, AutoCAD counts the division points beginning at the end of the curve nearest the pick point, so the results are affected by the way you select the objects.

To initiate the Ruled Surface command, choose **Toolbars** from the **Tools** pull-down menu, and then select **Surfaces**. The Surfaces toolbar appears as shown in Figure 6-13. (Note that all of the buttons on this tool-

Figure 6-13
Surfaces Toolbar

Ruled Surface

bar are not labelled—they are beyond the scope of this text.) Select the Ruled Surface button from the toolbar.

At the prompt

```
Select first defining curve:
```

pick an object, either a line or an arc. At the prompt

```
Select second defining curve:
```

pick another object. If the objects are open curves, lines, or arcs, the endpoints nearest the selection determine the orientation of the ruling lines.

Figure 6-14 illustrates ruled surfaces using lines as the defining curves. The two sets of lines in the drawing are of the same length and orientation. However, the lines were picked at points A and B in the image on the left, while they were picked at points E and H in the image on the right.

Figure 6-14
Ruled Surfaces Using Lines

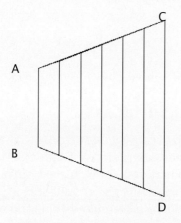 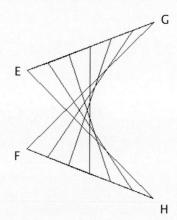

You can also use arcs as defining curves for ruled surfaces. As with lines, AutoCAD counts the division points beginning at the end of the arc nearest the pick point. Figure 6-15 illustrates how you can use the same defining curves but achieve different results by picking different portions of the curves.

Figure 6-15
Ruled Surfaces Using Arcs

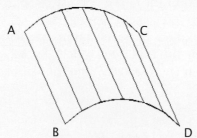 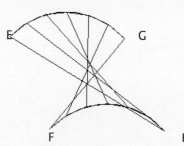

The ruled surfaces shown in Figure 6-16 use closed curves as the defining curves. It does not make any difference where you pick the closed curve. The results will always be the same, since the object has no endpoints.

Figure 6-16
**Ruled Surfaces Using
Closed Curves**

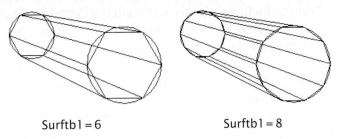

Surftb1 = 6   Surftb1 = 8

In the surfaces shown in Figures 6-14 and 6-15 and on the left side of Figure 6-16, AutoCAD used six panels to define the ruled surface. This default number, six, is a reasonable number to represent a surface for most applications. You can increase or decrease the number of panels by first choosing **System Variables, Set** from the **Options** pull-down menu. When prompted for the name of the variable you want to set, type SURFTAB1 and press (ENTER). Surftab1 controls the setting for surfaces with a single set of ruling lines. At the prompt

```
New value for SURFTAB1 <6>:
```

enter a new value and press (ENTER). Generally, a value between 6 and 12 is best since larger values will create a very dense-looking surface.

Now you have all of the tools you need to draw the wireframe model shown earlier in Figure 6-7.

6-7 DRAWING A WIREFRAME MODEL

Now you can apply the new skills you have just acquired to draw a wireframe model. While you will not be learning any new drawing or editing commands, you will learn a strategy that can be used for all wireframes. As you learn the strategy, you will learn more about the need for UCSs. You will have the opportunity to experiment with editing commands, such as Copy, Offset, and Trim, while working in three dimensions.

The wireframe that you will draw is the alignment block shown in Figure 6-17. The object is used to align two parts. The cylindrical projection

Figure 6-17
Alignment Block

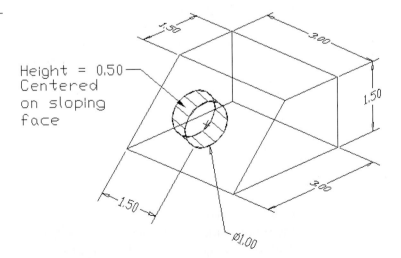

Try It

◆ Restore the TOP UCS, and try copying the circle. Observe that the copy is parallel to the top plane.

◆ Use Undo to remove the circle.

◆ Restore the INCLINE UCS, and copy the circle 0.5 units above the current XY plane.

◆ Add the ruling lines.

◆ Experiment with different Surftab1 settings to produce the ruled surface shown in Figure 6-21.

◆ Save the drawing as ALIGNBLK.

Figure 6-21
Completed Wireframe

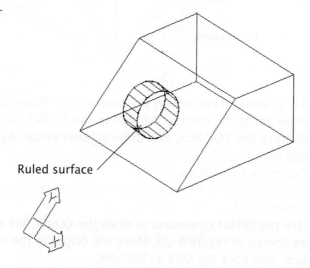

Ruled surface

6-8 CREATING ORTHOGRAPHIC VIEWS FROM WIREFRAMES

Orthographic views are the two-dimensional views used in drawings of objects that are to be manufactured. Orthographic views are visualized by a technique known as *orthographic projection*. An image of the object is projected onto a plane. If the plane is parallel to a principal plane in the object, the view is an orthographic view, as shown in Figure 6-22.

Imagine that the rectangular prism in Figure 6-22 is placed in a glass box. If the outline of the prism is projected up to the top surface of the glass box, the top view appears in that plane. The dashed lines with arrows represent the projection lines. Three of the six possible orthographic views—front, top, and right side—are arranged on the right of the figure. This is the standard arrangement. The other three views are the bottom, back, and left side views.

You can easily create standard orthographic views of the 3D wireframe model of the alignment block that you just completed. Formal engineering drawings typically consist of three orthographic views, each showing the device from a different viewpoint. You will create three orthographic views plus a special pictorial view of the alignment block.

You start creating orthographic views from a wireframe model by making blocks of the object. Recall that the Block command combines any number of drawn objects into a single entity. If you use the Block com-

Figure 6-22
**Illustrating
Orthographic Views**

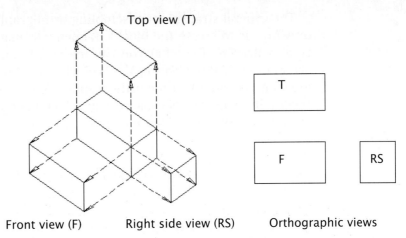

Top view (T)

Front view (F)   Right side view (RS)   Orthographic views

mand on a wireframe model, the image captured is the view of the object projected into the plane of the current UCS. In other words, you can create a block of the top view of the alignment block while the TOP UCS is current. The front and right side views are captured as blocks, while the FRONT and RIGHT UCSs, respectively, are current. You can then insert these blocks into a drawing and align them in the standard orthographic positions. You will need to remove the ruled surfaces and add the dimensions to complete the drawing.

Figure 6-23 shows three orthographic views of the alignment block. The 3D image of the wireframe is shown along with the three orthographic views. This image was created as a block using the UCS View option. The image captured by the Block command when the VIEW UCS is current is the actual image of the wireframe on the screen.

Figure 6-23
**Orthographic Views
from a Wireframe
Model**

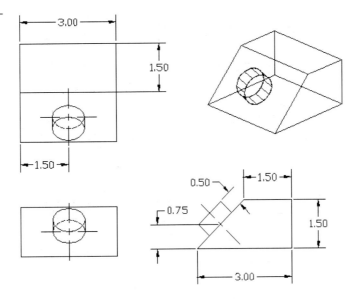

Try It ◆ Open the UCSWF drawing.
◆ Create blocks with each of the ABC, ABD, and AED UCSs current, plus a block with the UCS View option current.
◆ Change to the WCS and make a new layer.
◆ Insert the blocks back into the drawing on the new layer.

Figure 6-26
**Hyperbolic Paraboloid
Layout—Step 1**

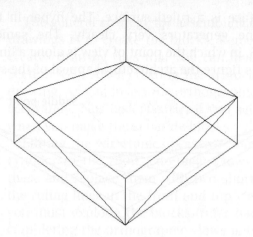

3. Make a Hand-drawn Sketch

Use Figure 6-25 as a sketch. You can use the strategy developed for wire-frame drawing to start this drawing. Draw a 40-by-40-by-16-foot box, and view it using 225-degree and 45-degree angles. Draw the four sloping lines that define the edges of the shell. Figure 6-26 shows the result of this step. Use Offset and Trim to finish the thickened front edges. Erase the extra construction lines. Draw the surface with two sets of ruling lines. Figure 6–27 shows the progress so far.

Figure 6-27
**Adding Thickened
Front Edges**

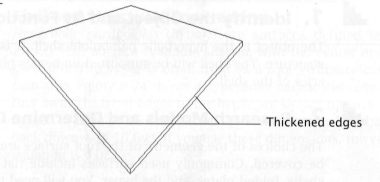

Thickened edges

Draw one set of ruling lines using two opposite edges as defining curves. After you have drawn one set of ruling lines, you cannot choose the other pair of edges as defining curves for the second set of ruling lines. The first set of ruling lines creates a mesh, similar to a block. The mesh obscures the edges of the shell. When you try to select an edge as a defining curve, AutoCAD selects the mesh instead. To solve the problem, you must move the first mesh, add the second set of ruling lines, and move the first mesh back again. Figure 6-28 shows the two sets of ruling lines with the first set temporarily moved.

4. Make Appropriate Screen Adjustments

Use Engineering units with 1 decimal place. Set the limits to 0,0 and 60',45'. Save these settings as a new prototype.

Figure 6-28
**Adding the Ruled
Surfaces**

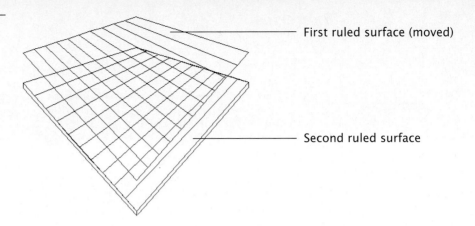

First ruled surface (moved)

Second ruled surface

 5. Draw, Print or Plot, and Save the File.

Draw the hypar as shown in Figure 6-25. Create three Wblocks, one using the UCS View setting, one with angle settings of 225 degrees and 0 degrees, and one with angle settings of 270 degrees and 90 degrees. Insert these blocks into a new drawing, and add text describing the images.

What If

What if the selection of the type of roof to use required four 20-by-20-foot hypars adjacent to one another? The outside points on the hypars are to be at 0-foot elevation and the common center point at 16 feet. How will you modify your approach to draw this new configuration?

SUMMARY

In this chapter you first learned how to create 3D objects using rotations, extrusions and primitive shapes. You then learned how to combine two objects by the Union, Subtract and Intersect commands. You learned how to change your viewpoint to see the objects in three dimensions. You learned how to control the screen icon, how to create User Coordinate Systems, and how to draw curved surfaces using the Ruled Surface command. You used these tools to draw wireframe models. Finally, you learned what orthographic drawings are and how to create them from wireframe models.

Key Words

defining curve	screen icon
extruded object	thickness
hyperbolic paraboloid (hypar)	three-dimensional (3D)
orthographic projection	User Coordinate System (UCS)
orthographic view	viewpoint
primitive	wireframe model (wireframe)
ruled surface	World Coordinate System (WCS)
ruling lines	

Exercises

Exercise 6-1
Tool Jig

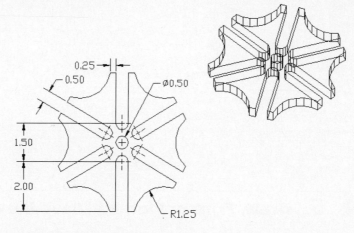

Make an extruded 3D drawing of the tool jig. The thickness is 0.5.

Exercise 6-2
Rocker Mechanism

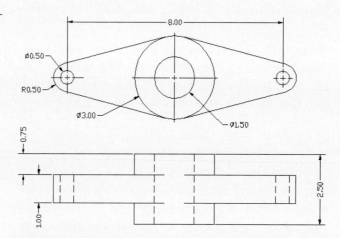

Make an extruded 3D drawing of the rocker mechanism.

Exercise 6-3
Gear

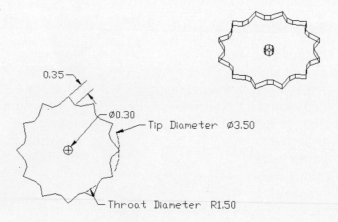

Make an extruded 3D drawing of the gear. The thickness is 0.2.

Exercise 6-4
Tool

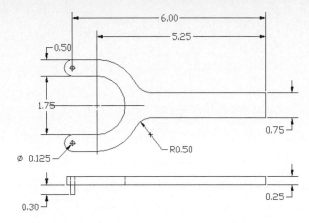

Make an extruded 3D drawing of the tool.

Make wireframe models of the devices in Exercises 6-5 through 6-9. Make orthographic drawings from the wireframe models. Add the dimensions and notes.

Exercise 6-5
Block

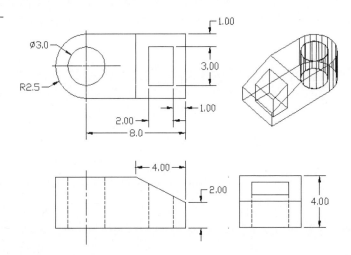

Exercise 6-6
Fin Plate

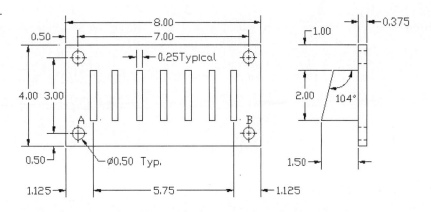

Exercise 6-7
Probe

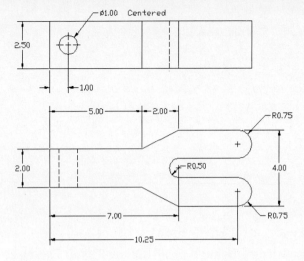

Exercise 6-8
Slide Plate

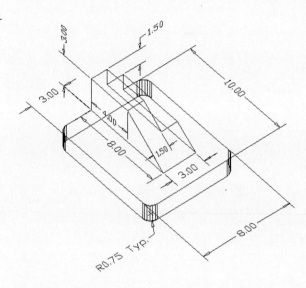

Exercise 6-9
Punch Guide

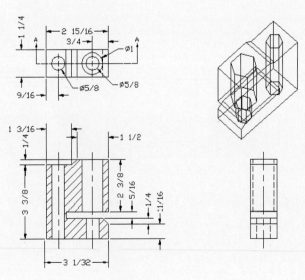

Index